Asperger Syndrome and Employment

What People with Asperger Syndrome Really Really Want

Sarah Hendrickx

Foreword by John Biddulph

Jessica Kingsley Publishers
London and Philadelphia

First published in 2009
by Jessica Kingsley Publishers
116 Pentonville Road
London N1 9JB, UK
and
400 Market Street, Suite 400
Philadelphia, PA 19106, USA

www.jkp.com

Copyright © Sarah Hendrickx 2009
Foreword copyright © John Biddulph 2009

Library of Congress Cataloging in Publication Data
A CIP catalog record for this book is available from the Library of Congress

British Library Cataloguing in Publication Data
A CIP catalogue record for this book is available from the British Library

ISBN 978 1 84310 677 7

Printed and bound in Great Britain by
Athenaeum Press, Gateshead, Tyne and Wear

Contents

Foreword

Employment is probably not the first thing that springs to mind when considering autism and Asperger Syndrome yet this compelling text by Sarah Hendrickx is persuasive and demanding in its argument. There is little doubt that there is both need and desire in many people on the autistic spectrum to succeed in the world of work. How they go about doing this is another matter: it is often a difficult path with many hurdles (intended or unintended) and challenges that do not always spring to mind in even the most sensitive and knowledgeable employer.

Through a crafted structure that is always insightful and often revelatory in nature, this book explores many issues through the experiences of the people who are on the receiving end. What should be a problem for employers (especially those who are not autistic) is precisely how people with AS receive this experience. Sadly, this is rarely the case and the open testimonies cleverly researched, collected and presented to us in this text reveal so much.

I am mindful of the 'square peg in a round hole' scenario. Yes, there are differences. Yes, people with AS do respond and react in different, surprising, often (given the chance) delightful ways so to engage with the needs of people with AS that are expressed in this book, it should be, at worst, a profitable experience and, at best, an experience that enriches both the workplace and the 'lifeplace' – the latter being a place in need of understanding and enrichment for people with AS.

The 'square peg in a round hole' scenario? Simple. Employers need to craft the round hole carefully and delicately so that the square peg will fit in it. Often, the outcome is a round hole that is made so big, the square peg just falls straight through, and worse still, there is no safety net or means of catching it on the other side.

This book should be read by employers, people with AS looking for work, people with AS in work but perhaps significantly, anyone needing to understand people on the autistic spectrum better. This need is a shared need and a shared responsibility. In short, it goes beyond this and becomes a responsibility, arguably a requirement of a decent, caring and responsible society.

Although feedback and debriefings are considered the norm after an unsuccessful interview, why shouldn't the interviewer or interviewing panel ask for feedback as to how they could have got precisely that information they want during the interviews by asking better questions, they can seem taken aback and almost affronted to receive similar information about their flawed interview techniques. Why is the assumption that the so called 'failed' interview is down to the interviewee and not the interviewer? Why are all the assumptions made about good working practice in need of a bit of a rethink? Why are the very things that autistic people are good at in terms of a potential job situation and highly valued in the world so rarely explored in an interview? Why do interviewers ask questions that are ridiculous to people with AS like "what do you think about equal opportunities?" Why do training and job access pathways tell people with AS to make a list (so far, so good) and create a Curriculum Vitae to 'sell' themselves (not so good now).

And why do employers spend too much time worrying about how to accommodate the differences and disabilities and not enough time facilitating the person with AS's strengths.

For an extraordinary insight into these issues and more: read on. It will change the way you think.

Introduction

Why are so few adults with Asperger Syndrome (AS) in employment?

This is ultimately the question that needs answering. Statistics for the numbers of those with AS in work vary – and will always be unreliable due to the large numbers of undiagnosed individuals – but are in the region of 15–20 per cent of the total known AS population (in the UK).

This is a remarkably low figure when we bear in mind that diagnostically AS comes with no learning disability – which is officially distinguished as having an IQ score significantly below the 'normal' range – and no physical disability in respect of mobility and accessing work premises. The educational achievements of people with AS range from none to those of professor; perhaps this is due more to the experience of school/university than to the differing intellectual abilities of those concerned.

This book attempts to explore the issues relating to work for those with AS. As in a previous publication, *Love, Sex and Long-Term Relationships – What People with Asperger Syndrome Really Really Want* (Hendrickx 2008), I have called upon a number of adults with AS to share their thoughts, wishes and experiences on this topic. Too often the well-meaning advice of 'experts' replaces the first-hand knowledge of individuals themselves. I hope that the huge wealth of experience, awareness and honesty shared by those with AS who contributed speaks for itself for the most part. My motivation for working in this way is to try to expose practitioners, professionals and those with AS to the wide range of opinions and experiences that exist across this population. Often we meet and work with just one person with AS and assume that we know how it is for everyone with the condition. This is absolutely not the case, as each person has their own unique combination and profile of AS characteristics, but without access to larger numbers of those affected, we cannot broaden our judgement and knowledge. By presenting views from a number of people with AS, I hope to partially achieve exactly that. Or at least introduce the concept that this is not a homogenous group – pigeon-hole at your peril! Also, in having fewer social contacts, it may be hard for some with AS to find individuals with whom to share their experience of life, which is isolating and sometimes depressing. I hope that by opening up the worlds of others with AS, that sense of 'no one else feels the way I do' may be diminished. You are undoubtedly not alone; I hope that this fact gives some solace in a tough world.

My hunch when considering writing this book, was that those with AS work for different reasons than the majority of people. I suspected that motivation was less dependent on social status, progression and financial gain, and more to do with personal interests and enjoyment and everything to do with maintaining low stress levels. For some this is certainly shown to be the case. I feel that considering the motivations of others can enable us to think more clearly about ourselves and the methods that we use to persuade people to enter into a world (the workplace) that may have little, or at least a different, meaning to them than it does for us. This will have an impact not only on those who provide workplace training, careers advice and employment support, but also on those who design the policies which are designed to encourage a desire for employment in the currently unemployed. If the fundamental understanding of the person's reality is not addressed, then it's like trying to reward a vegetarian with a hamburger; there simply is no motivation (and at worst it may be a de-motivator).

Additionally, there is often the inherently mistaken assumption, just because a person has a whole bunch of qualifications and no apparent physical or mental disability, that they are able to hold down a job. This is certainly not the case for many people I have met with AS. Being smart doesn't mean that you can negotiate the complex social minefield of an office environment, organise shopping, laundry and bill-paying, so as to be healthy and presentable enough to work, or travel on a crowded bus to get there. If a person finds it hard to manage the rest of life, they are unlikely to be able to hold down a job. The focus of many generic job search programmes seems to measure people's ability to work by a set of criteria that don't meet the needs of those with AS, and does not question the skill levels in other areas of life. Consequently these programmes fail, and will continue to do so, unless they change, and learn what this group needs to achieve employment success. Current employment rates of the AS population testify to the lack of success of many of these programmes.

For the data from those with AS, I contacted people who kindly contributed to my previous book (Hendrickx 2008), several of whom agreed to contribute again. Twenty-five people with AS (diagnosed or self-diagnosed) completed questionnaires or were interviewed: 3 women and 22 men. The age range of those participating was 21 years to 75 years, and just over 64 per cent of the sample was under the age of 50. Over 70 per cent of those questioned had degree-level qualifications or higher. Four people were unemployed, which makes a figure of 84 per cent employed. Therefore this is a totally unrepresentative sample for the AS population. In the world of this book, most people with AS have a job!

Enormous thanks go to those people for their continuing support for my often confusingly worded questions. This group are perhaps atypical to the majority of those with AS in that many of them have found successful employment and, owing to not receiving a diagnosis until later in life, have done so without support. It is interesting to note what has made this possible for them and how this could be replicated more widely to help others. Others in my professional and personal life have also contributed along with new volunteers gathered from various sources, for which I am also grateful. The majority of the views contributed are from men with AS, as they were the people who came forward to do so, but the employment issues seem to be universal, regardless of gender. The gender and ages (the decade rather than the year, to ensure anonymity) of those commenting have been added to give some context to their responses, but there were a lot of similar experiences and statements which recurred time and time again, regardless of age or gender.

I have also been able to consult with several service users of ASpire (www.aspire.bh-impetus.org), the project that I work for, which supports adults with AS through the provision of volunteer mentors. Most of the interviews with ASpire users were carried out by Sam Bond and Didier Montillaud, who both volunteer for the project. They have kindly undertaken to interview individuals with AS in order to glean as much detail as possible as to their insights and experiences. Didier has also contributed an extended case study to the book, focused on the experiences of both employer and employee, to provide both sides of the story. It has been great to have this external input into the research aspect of the book – a first for me and hugely valued and appreciated.

I have also been fortunate enough to make contact with Specialisterne (www.specialisterne.dk), a company based in Copenhagen, Denmark, which employs a workforce consisting predominantly of individuals with autistic spectrum disorders (ASD), mostly AS. This is presented as a case study and a model for how other organisations seeking to empower those with AS in retaining employment could operate. Thorkil Sonne, the founder, has been most helpful in providing me with information, as have two members of his staff, who completed the questionnaire. I can verify Thorkil's belief that those with ASD are the same the world over – well, they certainly seem to have very similar experiences and desires in Denmark and the UK, anyway. I would also like to thank David Perkins from the National Autistic Society's Prospects employment programme (www.nas.org.uk/prospects) for taking the time with speak to me.

There are a number of excellent publications on AS and employment already available. They are mostly advisory and practical in nature and designed to provide employers and employees with the tools to build a successful working relationship. This book is as much concerned with the 'why' and the 'what' as the 'how' and so, I hope, complements these others rather than replicates them. I have particularly enjoyed Roger N. Meyer's *Asperger Syndrome Employment Workbook* (Meyer 2001). Roger writes in such a straightforward and easy-to-understand manner. He also has a very real and personal awareness of the issues involved for those with AS in finding and keeping work. Roger's book is very practical, requiring those with AS seeking work to log all of their experience and skills and reflect on their requirements – often not a natural AS attribute! The book also includes a fabulously comprehensive list of AS characteristics, which goes beyond the obvious and widely known ('stilted or pedantic conversation style') to the more subtle but enormously important ('difficulty understanding the relationship between a personal action and its consequence').

I hope that this book reveals a new understanding of the reality for those with AS and helps us to make adjustments to that reality in order to ensure that as many people as possible with AS are supported to succeed in work that befits their abilities and intelligences.

1

How Asperger Syndrome Affects Employment / Everything

It would not be an understatement to say that Asperger Syndrome affects everything. It has an impact on each and every area of an individual's life (and often the lives of those around them), so it is impossible to separate employment from the rest. There are so many issues to contend with before work can be contemplated – eating, dressing, leaving the house, paying the bills, answering the phone…and so on. And that is without even finding, selecting, applying and successfully securing a job. Employment itself throws up specific challenges, which mainly involve doing things that you may not want to do, in a place not of your choosing, with people you may not like, in a way that you may not wish to. None of these activities are necessarily favoured by people with AS.

I think it is useful to have a basic understanding of the characteristics and likely implications of AS, before considering their impact on the employment prospects of an individual with the condition. This chapter looks at what people report about how AS affects them generally, and gives a brief overview of the characteristics of the condition. These comments are not restricted solely to work-related issues. It is worth noting that these individuals come from a range of backgrounds and personal circumstances and demonstrate the diversity of the AS diagnosis. Individuals were asked to note any other health conditions which could also affect their ability to work and function, as I felt these might have an effect (for some) on their employment capabilities, since having

AS does not preclude one from other health conditions. I have also covered the issue of anxiety in the discussion on AS characteristics, as it is a big part of life with the condition for many people, although not part of the diagnostic criteria. We will see that having to live with AS is enough to make anyone feel anxious. The responses from those who answered the questions will testify to this fact.

There are other publications which feature more detailed information on diagnostic criteria and manifestations, most notably Tony Attwood's *Complete Guide to Asperger Syndrome* (Attwood 2006), and I shall only provide a brief overview here. Some of this generic AS information has featured previously in *Asperger Syndrome and Alcohol: Drinking to Cope?* (Tinsley and Hendrickx 2008).

AS is characterised diagnostically by three main areas of difference from expected norms of behaviour: social interaction, communication and language, and lack of flexibility in thought and behaviour. Environmental sensitivity, although not mentioned specifically in the various diagnostic criteria for AS, is often said to feature in most people's experience of having AS.

Possible characteristics of someone with this complex condition are as follows.

Social interaction

- Differences in the ability to read social cues and messages, particularly nonverbal gestures, which others seem to intuitively 'know'.

- May appear to be naïve, tactless or arrogant by saying or doing the 'wrong' thing socially.

- Difficulty appreciating thoughts, feelings and opinions of other people as being potentially different to one's own.

- May talk about one subject at length and lack the ability to recognise (or care) whether others are listening or interested.

- Failing to adhere to social rules, which often results in ridicule, aggression or exclusion.

Someone with AS may typically appear to be awkward in social situations, not picking up on unspoken 'rules'. They may behave in a socially or professionally inappropriate way and find it hard to understand why their behaviour has offended or bothered others. For example, someone might mention how much weight a female colleague has put on recently, or speak very loudly about a personal issue and not be able to consider that others may find sensitive topics uncomfortable – he/she would only be able to see the matter from their own viewpoint. Some people talk to themselves quite loudly and find it stressful to silence this inner voice externally. None of these behaviours is done deliberately to annoy or offend; the person simply does not have abilities as advanced in this area as other (non-AS) people do:

> To put it bluntly, I suck at social situations! I am very uncomfortable in situations with people I don't know; even if there are people there as well that I do know. The only thing that can make me lose all unease I have in most any social situation, is if the conversation is about role-playing games. Then I can talk for hours without noticing anything else around me. (male, 20s)

> Hard to go to the library as I talk to myself a lot. Since I have stopped drinking, I talk to myself constantly. (male, 20s)

> I find that in social situations, I don't always know what's going on, so I might sometimes begin a topic of conversation which is completely unrelated to the current flow of conversations. I tell inappropriate jokes. I lie a lot but I am not sure if it's to do with my AS. I lie about my achievements. I feel low about how little I have achieved at my age. I don't like to deal with serious matters. I don't know what to chat about with girls. (male, 20s)

> Finding it more difficult to build social relationships because of my unease in company of strangers. All feels unnatural and forced (but not always). Some intellectual effort required. (male, 40s)

I have somewhat learned to copy my wife in difficult interactions, particularly with officialdom. (male, 60s)

My social understanding [is] nearly non-existent. It's entirely based on analysis and guesstimating correct responses! (male, 30s)

I don't like small talk. I can never get the hang of it and it always feels so fake. I still feel dirty when I say 'how are you?', and I still find myself stopping to think before answering that question if it is asked of me, even though the other person is just expecting me to say 'fine'. (male, 33)

Social skills have improved thanks to my wife's 'training' and 'nagging' – her word. For instance, if I went to lunch with relatives, I saw nothing wrong in closing my eyes and having a nap in their company. This caused a great deal of tension between me and my wife. (male, 60s)

Meeting people I don't know is a bloody nightmare. I get told off for not talking to strangers or saying anything to them except 'hello', 'goodbye'. Apparently I should be saying things like 'Have you worked here long?' This is what I've been told to say, mind, rather than the things I'd like to talk about – 'What's your take on Bush's stance on the Kyoto protocol and his attitude towards the UN Climate Control Summit?'…Surprisingly I do quite well if I'm in chat rooms on the internet and I can talk about interesting subjects and have made a couple of close friends of both sexes through that. That might be because I know a lot about everything and become an arbiter of all knowledge. Anything from the genetic make-up of the coffee plant (Robusta vs. Arabica) to how to tie someone up. (male, 40s)

Small talk is quite problematic. In part because it seems to me as though it is lying. I am told that conversation is like a game of tennis; one person asks a question and the other answers and returns a question. If someone asks me how I am, and I ask them back in return, then where do you go from here? To me, this end of the line is game, set and match. Also I do not like tennis and am not very good at it. Conversation, like tennis, is something I would – by choice – avoid. (female, 20s)

Not always aware of how others feel and I fake it by mirroring back to people what I see as their emotional state. I often get this wrong and that causes problems. (male, 50s)

Socially, there are times I don't fit in, and I just don't get it. (male, 30s)

Communication and language

- Difficulty reading nonverbal signals, body language and facial expression.
- Difficulty understanding subtleties of humour, subtext and non-literal meanings of spoken language.
- Needing very precise instructions and not being overloaded with information.
- Failing to communicate accurately, resulting in misunderstanding, stress and exclusion.
- Using precise and literal language and requiring this for understanding.

A person with AS may find the language and emotions on the face difficult to 'read'. They may struggle to make eye contact, finding it pointless or overwhelming. They may use very pedantic and literal language, communicating in a very precise manner. Luke Beardon (Beardon and Edmonds 2008) makes the point that those with AS may not be misinterpreting information, but may be too precise or accurate in their understanding. He asks the question: how can this be a bad thing? The point here is that it takes more than one person to communicate effectively and that if we were all clear and exact in our communication, there would be no problem. Those with AS may also require information to be presented to them in a similarly detailed and exact way in order to understand it. If the understanding is not there, the person may be paralysed and have no idea what to do or how to react. This can lead to feelings of inadequacy, stupidity and low confidence. Their thinking tends to be logical, and their decisions to be based on rational thought rather than emotions or feelings.

> I mistake sarcasm for seriousness and treat it as such, i.e. I have in the past gone away and worried all night about something that someone said. Not realising or even entertaining the possibility that it was either sarcasm or a joke. This leaves me vulnerable to being a source of amusement. (female, 20s)

> I cannot read people, so with outsiders, I tend to acquiesce. (male, 70s)

> I look like I am staring at people when in fact I am looking at the pattern on the wallpaper or something else behind them. (male, 20s)

> When listening to a conversation, I pipe up that I know about something and just go on and on and they get pissed off and bored with me. (male, 20s)

> I get a bit paranoid as I can't really tell if people like me or not, so I worry. If they make friendly approaches, it's fine. If I have to approach them, it's difficult. (female, 20s)

> If individuals with ASD [autistic spectrum disorder] have an impaired theory of mind, and therefore do not read people and their actions, expressions, intentions, feelings so well, then this is compounded by the fact that I also think that everyone else has possession of exactly the same facts as I do. I make no (or only intellectual and limited) concession for the fact that another person may not know or see what I see. (female, 20s)

Lack of flexibility in thought and behaviour

- A need for own routines and preferred ways of doing things.

- Limited interests and conversational topics.

- Dislike of change, variety, surprises and spontaneity.

- Rigid thought patterns which find new concepts, planning, consequences and abstract thought difficult.

- Inability to tolerate flexibility can be stressful, anxiety-provoking and create difficulties within social relationships, as the person may be seen as selfish and uncaring of others' needs.

- Black-and-white thinking – seeing only one or two options to any situation, an all-or-nothing approach to life with difficulty in perceiving other options or degrees.

- Difficulties with short-term memory, organisation and planning.

Managing unpredictable situations or changes to routines can be very stress-provoking for someone with AS. Due to their reduced ability to understand all of the social interactions around them, they may cling to safe, known situations and routines in order to maintain a sense of control and familiarity in a world which feels chaotic and illogical. This can result in a narrow focus in both thought and action, where the individual is unable to consider other perspectives or behaviours outside what is already known. The person may, for example, insist on eating the same food every day, sit in the same seat on the bus and become agitated when this is not possible, and find it difficult to manage changes at work or home. The tendency towards black-and-white thinking may result in unrealistic choices and perspectives. For example, someone in a relationship may feel that the relationship must be perfect and that any disagreement is a sign that it is a failure and should be abandoned. 'If it's not perfect, it must be terrible' is the thinking, and the ability to consider other, positive aspects is less developed.

I don't think that my AS gets in the way of the things I decide to do. However, I need to know in advance if there will be changes in my plans or any other things I am due to do, otherwise I get annoyed and anxious. (male, 40s)

I prefer to adhere to a predictable routine, and find changes quite hard to handle. I often spend a lot of time in my room, and am happy to do so. (male, 40s)

Routines – if someone else interrupts my routine, it buggers me totally. (male, 20s)

I do not vary my routine and if I do, then that produces anxiety and I withdraw, which does not impress my wife or daughters. (male, 50s)

I need to have some personal routines in my life, but also I need changes often, or I lose my ability to concentrate and focus on much of anything. My DVDs are in a specific order and my books as well. If something isn't where its supposed to be then I get frustrated and slowly, almost unnoticeably builds up this frustration until I get depressed and can't really do much of anything. (male, 20s)

I need to schedule many of my daily activities otherwise I won't get things done. I mostly interact with people as part of my scheduled routines (e.g. work). I rarely connect with other people spontaneously. (male, 30s)

Used to find holidays difficult – needed time to adjust to the change, by which time it was usually time to go home! (male, 60s)

I get overloaded very easily. If my routine is blown out of the water I am completely out of sorts. (male, 30s)

[My social life] is constrained by routine and order. I do not want to break my routine, and do not want to have to meet the NT [neuro-typical/non-AS] world in the pub unless I absolutely have to. (male, 20s)

I have the usual problems with routine. My diet is comprised of whatever I am currently stuck on. Sometimes this being stuck will last a few days, sometimes over a year. Similarly with clothes, I have little insight, interest or knowledge of fashion and this, combined with problems with labels and seams and certain types of material, make clothes an area of difficulty. Well, it's only difficult for me when something wears out and I have to try and find something else either identical or near to identical. (female, 20s)

Once I get into a certain subject I am there until I exhaust it or it exhausts me. I love to know how things work. (male, 20s)

My home is always messy, and I don't eat right because I can't be bothered to cook. There are always more interesting things to do, and the mundane stuff always falls by the wayside. (male, 40s)

Time management. Tired and stressed easily. Stuff gets over-whelming sometimes. I don't like things I don't understand – new places, new contexts. I know there will be rules and I don't know what they are, especially if I'm on my own and there's no one to ask or copy. (female, 20s)

I need mini goals, or specific chores such as 'put away the dishes' or 'load the dishwasher'. When I'm told to 'clean the kitchen', this is a broad request. Every little job has the same priority to me. I literally wind up walking around the kitchen in circles saying 'x needs doing, but I can't because y needs doing, but I can't because z needs doing, but I can't because x needs to be done'. (male, 30s)

I need to have my own personal framework of organisation – best described not as 'routines' but rather are idiosyncratic and complex organisations of 'stuff' (documents, objects, physical space) – which provides resources for my day-to-day ad-hoc flow of activity. I depend very much on these toolkits and layouts of workspace. (male, 60s)

Some people find that their short-term memory lets them down and this can be very frustrating and increase stress when important things are forgotten:

> I need to keep my daily things (keys, wallet, belt, jacket, shoes, etc.) in their specific place or I will forget them. (male, 30s)

> My biggest problem is with memory and fatigue. I am slow at getting things done. I am sometimes overwhelmed. I manage mother's money as well as mine. All these activities are difficult and make me tired… Managing the checkout at the supermarket is difficult and stressful. Multitasking at any rate is difficult and potentially stressful. (male, 50s)

Environmental sensitivity

- Limited range of tolerance for certain noises, smells, textures, physical touch, etc.

- Need and strong preference for certain noises, smells, textures, physical touch, etc.

- Inability to tolerate/do without certain stimuli can result in isolation and withdrawal from environmental stressors.

Environments which are too stressful may be avoided by the person with AS as the sensory input is just too overwhelming for them to manage. Certain noises or smells can be intolerable and painful. This may include travelling to work on a crowded bus or having to sit in an office which they find unbearably hot or cold, due to differences in temperature tolerance. If avoidance is not an option (because it is the workplace for example), other coping strategies may be put into place. Alcohol may be one of the options for managing this stress and confusion. For some, the effort of coping with a working environment that they find difficult means that there is no spare energy to manage a social life or outside activities as well, the effects of any individual stressors being cumulative. The remainder of the person's time is spent alone, 'recharging' from the day.

I am aware of anything and everything around me, always. I very much dislike strong light, especially sunlight, and also loud noise, monotonous sounds, and disharmonic sounds are very uncomfortable to me. I am unable to ignore such noise and it disrupts any form of concentration or relaxation I might require at the given time. (male, 20s)

My need for solitude overrides almost everything. (male, 30s)

I prefer doing things alone, and living alone, and in general being alone. Being around other people is just too stressful. (male, 30s)

Sensory – family social occasions – kissing and hugging thing freaks me out. It's my space and my body, leave me alone. (male, 20s)

I always used to describe noisy/crowded places as feeling claustrophobic, though now I realise it's a combination of noise and too many people. (male, 40s)

I cannot go outside without having some music with me. Without it I am simply unable to filter all the sensory inputs that bombard me when I ride the bus or go shopping. I never go outside just to take a walk; I need to have a purpose for going outside. If I do not have my MP3 player with me, I get extremely exhausted within a very short amount of time. In most extreme cases, where there are many people around me all the time, like in a crowded supermarket, I react similar to panic attacks and must go home immediately. (male, 20s)

I don't like fluorescent lights, and the tags in clothing drive me nuts. I always cut them out. (male, 20s)

I hate going into crowded shops and have a habit of going at one or two in the morning when I reckon they'll be almost empty. A quick in-and-out is OK, but if it takes more than half an hour or so I've been known to abandon trolleys at the checkout if it's too busy. (male, 40s)

> I do not have good fine motor skills. Handwriting is a disaster and when writing I tend to go crosseyed and have to keep refocusing. (male, 50s)

> Eye contact is painful. I am told that it is something that needs to improve. But, when I look at people's eyes, I have to look away. The sense of it being too intense, painful and detrimental to my ability to talk with them, is something that I find difficult to explain. I am not shy or shifty. It is just intolerable. I work in a busy hospital and one of the five basic rules of providing good care for each patient is maintaining eye contact. Therefore my struggle is noticed and commented upon in terms of me not meeting the baseline standards required. I find this unfair. (female, 20s)

One's own awareness of personal differences in each of these areas – usually learned from the reactions of others – can cause anxiety, stress and depression. Some people with AS consider the sensory aspects of their condition to be the most debilitating. When one is unable to cope with the physical environment, it is exhausting and all-consuming. Attention, communication and productivity are impossible when in extreme discomfort. If you can recall a time when you were in considerable pain, we can empathise with this; the pain takes over all other physical and mental functions. This is the experience of some people with AS throughout normal daily activities. These sensory experiences are very real and need to be addressed in the workplace, as failure to do so is in effect discrimination.

Anxiety

Although anxiety is not among the defining diagnostic criteria of AS, we can see that the characteristics briefly outlined above can reasonably be expected to cause high levels of anxiety, stress and depression in those who experience them – but what about further evidence of a connection?

Tony Attwood, a leading authority on Asperger Syndrome, sees those with Asperger Syndrome managing anxiety as an everyday part of their lives, and some of these people go on to develop anxiety disorders, including social anxiety disorder. He suggests that current research shows that over half of adolescents with Asperger Syndrome have a secondary mood or affective disorder (such as depression or anxiety) (Attwood 2006).

> Social phobia, or social anxiety disorder, would be expected to be relatively common for those with Asperger Syndrome, especially in the teenage and adult years when they are more acutely aware of their confusion in social situations, of making social mistakes, and possibly suffering ridicule. (Attwood 2006, p.140)

> I am anxious all the time because I don't know what's going to happen. I have a lot of sensory hypersensitivities, which I cope with through sensory routines (similar to OCD or Tourette's). I find it hard to tell how I feel or what I want, so I make arbitrary decisions. I feel isolated in social situations. (female, 20s)

> I have had panic attacks in the past when I was in unfamiliar places without a familiar person to make me feel normal. (female, 20s)

While not suggesting that AS and social anxiety disorders are the same thing, we suggest that some people diagnosed with social anxiety may in fact have AS and that their social fears are not entirely unjustified. The person with AS may have a legitimate fear of social errors, as they may be aware that their skills in this area have let them down in the past. Both those with AS and those with social anxiety disorder will avoid social situations for fear of humiliation and/or embarrassment at 'getting it wrong'. One man with Asperger Syndrome explains this:

> It's not so much 'getting it wrong' but a matter of accepting (or knowing) time after time that you don't know what to do and have no hope of 'getting it right' so its easier not to bother. (male, 30s)

Features of social anxiety disorder include:

- fear or anxiety in relation to people, being near or having to interact with others

- fear of judgement or criticism by other people, which may result in being hyper-sensitive to comment from others

- dread and panic before certain situations and potential replaying or ruminating on the event afterwards

- physical symptoms such as shaking, nausea and raised heart rate.

This gives a pretty gloomy look to life with AS and also begins to give a sense of the kinds of difficulties a person may have in dealing with the complications and stresses of work as well as coping with a life outside, but it is important to add that many adults with AS are carving their own path through this complex and confusing world and finding solutions and environments which suit them. Some people find that reading books on body language or learning social scripts for conversations is helpful. One person listened to football scores on the radio, despite having no interest in the sport, as he worked out that this was a topic commonly discussed by men in social situations and having this knowledge enabled him to join in. Some of these solutions may be unconventional, but unconventionality is often an overlooked AS skill.

Although not necessarily work-related, it is clear to see how any one of the issues mentioned above will have a real impact on the person's capacity to cope with daily employment. The mental energy required to deal with short-term memory difficulties, not understanding social situations and maintaining routines in a flexible environment means that there is much less available to be spent on the job itself.

Other health issues

AS often comes with a range of other conditions in tow, often as a result of misdiagnosis or co-morbidity. These tend to be related differences such as dyslexia, epilepsy, dyspraxia, anxiety, depression, or other mental health conditions. I have met and read of a number of people who have been wrongly diagnosed with (and medicated for) schizophrenia. The youngest of these was only 26 years old, so this is not something which only occurred in the past. Two respondents experienced alcoholism, which may have some connection with the difficulties of managing the stress and anxiety associated with AS for some. This is discussed further in *Asperger Syndrome and Alcohol* (Tinsley and Hendrickx 2008). There may be a gut connection with autistic spectrum conditions, and incidences of coeliac disease (gluten intolerance), lactose intolerance and gastric conditions, such as irritable bowel syndrome (IBS), do seem to be above average levels, in my experience. General anxiety was often an accepted by-product of life with Asperger Syndrome.

> Nothing more drastic than Asperger Syndrome and the anxiety that it engenders that negatively makes a mess of my life in a health way. (male, 30s)

> Epilepsy, alcoholism, stress/anxiety/depression, physical problems relating to alcohol withdrawal, dyslexia. (male, 29)

> I have ADHD and take medication for this (Ritalin)... Ritalin has changed my life. It has also isolated and in some ways rendered more visible the effects of ASD on my behaviour and in my life. (female, 20s)

> I have ME (myalgic encephalopathy/chronic fatigue syndrome), asthma, allergies and rhinitis. My state of mind has an effect on my physical health... I am now trying to manage my mental and physical health with diet. (male, 30s)

> Dyslexia and AS. This combination may have been why I had trouble making friends. Not only was I 'not getting it' (AS), I was also a bit strange (dyslexia). I have a tic which involves swishing my hair, but no one notices as they think I am just swishing my hair. (female, 20s)

> Depression. It hit me really hard last year when I found out I had AS and my wife freaked out. We are now getting divorced and she's moved back to [country] with our daughter. Depression is the worst imaginable, because it saps the very life essence out of you. When you can't even muster the energy to get out of bed, you can't do anything else either, except just lie there staring blankly at a wall. (male, 30s)

The experiences shared in this chapter provide a broad overview of the types of difficulties experienced by a number of adults with AS. Some of these people work at very high levels within their occupations and have become experts in their chosen field. Some of those who are high achievers in their careers have the most significant daily issues to overcome and must be working very hard continuously to cope with them. For others, going to work is simply intolerable, and only adds to feelings of lack of worth and low self-esteem. Those who have found successful employment give some degree of hope to others who would like to work, but have yet to find the support and environment that will allow them to reach their potential.

2

When Work Doesn't Work

I'm overwhelmed by having to work and dedicating my time to this activity that I feel disassociated from. It drains me completely and I feel unable to do anything else. I'm continually wishing away the working period of my life. Let me retire right now so as I can go and do the things I want, or rather not to have to feel manacled to something that feels as though it completely controls my life. I occasionally hide in the toilet at work just to get an injection of solitude. (Hendrickx and Newton 2007, p.83)

These words come from Keith Newton, who loves what he does (software engineering) and wouldn't want to do any other type of work – unless it was no work at all! He finds the load of all that is required of him in the workplace so exhausting that he has little time and energy outside of it for anyone or anything else. Keith sees no one in a social capacity outside of work from one week to the next, does nothing during his evenings and has never been able to tolerate living with anyone. He requires long periods of 'de-stressing' time alone. He has no friends, no social life or activities at which he meets people. He finds organisation, processing of information and relationships with people difficult. He feels unable to share his life or home with anyone while he has to go to work to earn a living. He does not eat a balanced diet because he rarely has the energy or inclination to cook meals for himself. This is because he has AS and goes to work. These are quite major limitations but quite typical of those faced by others with AS. The strain of dealing with the external world takes Keith to the limit of his capacity:

> Work takes up a third of my days during the working week.
> This is not extraordinary and is no more than most working
> people. Yet the interruption it places upon my time is such an
> imposition that I find trying to arrange anything else for the
> remainder of my day difficult. It's so hard to manage with all
> these things in my head at the same time. (Hendrickx and
> Newton 2007, p.83)

To the outside world, Keith would be described as 'mildly' affected by AS
(although I personally disagree with this measurement of severity of
affect based on external presentation of behaviour), as he has a successful
career (consisting of only two jobs over a 15-year period, both doing the
same work) and his own home, although the isolated and limited nature
of his life outside work seems to indicate quite a significant impairment in
functioning. Often people like Keith go unnoticed because they are able
to get through what is required of them at work, but the invisible aspect is
the amount of decompressing time require to maintain it. I have met
others whose coping strategies for managing working, socialising and AS
have included alcohol and drug abuse to a life-threatening degree. Matt
Tinsley describes his alcohol use as a means of 'numbing' the anxiety of
undiagnosed AS in *Asperger Syndrome and Alcohol: Drinking to Cope?*
(Tinsley and Hendrickx 2008, p.86):

> I know that I would not have been able to keep the jobs that I
> have had in my life if I had not used alcohol to give me the
> tools to do so. Most people would say that drinking alcohol
> while working was unequivocally a bad thing and that being
> sober makes you a much more effective employee. In my
> case, however, I firmly believe that I was only able to do the
> jobs and also to put on the act of normality through subli-
> mating my real self through alcohol.

The employment rate of those with disabilities varies according to the
type of disability affecting the individual. The following groups are likely
to contain people with AS and demonstrate that employment rates are
very low across all of these conditions. Obviously, these statistics cover
the whole range of severity of mental health. Of those with depression,
22.2 per cent are in employment. Of those with mental illness, phobia

and panics, only 10.4 per cent are in employment (Smith and Twomey 2001). A report by the National Autistic Society (Barnard, Prior and Potter 2000) found that 20 per cent of adults with autism were in paid work, with 30 per cent in unpaid (voluntary) work. The study stated that 59 per cent of adults with autism would like to be working and only 13 per cent would not. Reasons that people gave as barriers to going to work included: coping with social side of work, not being sure what they would be able to do as a job, the lack of a support worker, and negative perceptions of employers. It is not unusual for adults with AS to have a 'chequered employment history of several low paid jobs' (Beardon and Edmonds 2008).

I do not wish to stipulate 'good' and 'bad' work roles and environments for someone with AS, as each individual will have their personal skills and preferences, but some scenarios seem to be more favourable than others. Any work situation which involves high levels of stress is likely to be unmanageable for someone with AS, who is already dealing with elevated stress levels as part of their constant experience of life. Job roles which involve pressure and constant demands should perhaps be avoided, or at least entered into with extreme caution, by those with AS, as they may not have the reserves to manage the requirements of the job without harming themselves. Giles Harvey (Beardon and Edmonds 2008) provides a list of jobs which he feels that those with AS would have a higher or lesser likelihood of success at. His high risk of failure list includes air traffic controller, ambulance driver, high/secondary school teacher, fire officer and salesperson. Harvey also advises avoiding working in large corporate headquarters due to the amount of work stress, workload and the 'ruthlessness of the managers'. More successful jobs may be roles where team-working is not a large part of the job, where instructions and expectations are clear and the environment is not stress-provoking in itself. Even so, sometimes situations can arise from unexpected and unlikely circumstances, which no one would have predicted. For example, I once supported an employer with regard to one of their staff members with AS who had put in a formal complaint against a colleague who had jokingly called him a 'lazy bastard' and slapped him on the back. His complaint was that he felt he had been verbally and physically abused. His colleague's intention was to engage him in light-hearted banter, which is typical of certain workplaces. He had not understood the very confusing subtleties of social interaction whereby it is generally felt to be socially acceptable for someone to behave like this in certain situations, but entirely inappropriate in others. He had taken the unwelcome physical contact and abusive words literally and had been unable to attribute context to the situation. He had no means of distinguishing one situation from another and was very offended at the behaviour he experienced. It was very difficult for his employers to know how to handle the situation, which did not really warrant disciplinary proceedings for the colleague involved, who was not acting maliciously, but also made it necessary to acknowledge the genuine grievance of the person with AS. The solution was to develop a set of guidelines for how the person with AS preferred to be treated: no physical contact, no jokes and no banter, as he was unable to understand them and found them stressful and offensive. Training was recommended for all staff on AS awareness, but only with the consent of the employee.

The following comments are focused on aspects of jobs which had not worked out well at all for those interviewed.

Difficult job roles and workplaces

There seems to be a range of common issues at work that those with AS find difficult. The idea of being given enough instruction to understand the task and yet enough autonomy to do it in one's own way was an important point mentioned by several people. Jobs which involved interaction with people, including elements of required socialising, were the most stressful of all for those questioned. Often entry-level jobs, such as supermarket cashier, waiting staff or office admin work all require interaction, flexibility and a highly sensory environment. These are the job roles that some with AS are expected to perform, but are the least likely to succeed in.

> I didn't especially enjoy working on the checkout because I didn't know what to say to the customers. It didn't seem enough that you checked out their shopping, some people expected you to chat to them. I noticed other people alongside me doing this, and the odd laugh, and I just knew I couldn't do it. (Edmonds and Beardon 2008, p.44)

There is also a sense in some of the following comments of a known characteristic of AS, dislike of authority. Several people comment on knowing more than their managers and it is unlikely that they would have been able to conceal this effectively. This attitude, although probably correct in many cases, does not help to make friendships and effective working relationships. Those in positions of authority like others to believe that they deserve to be there. They will expect to be treated accordingly and with respect, for no other reason than their superior status. There is a known tendency of those with AS to treat everyone equally, or to give respect only where they personally feel that it is due – not where society says it should be directed.

> Working in banking where I tended to manipulate customers to sell banking products and found this was not an enjoyable role. (male, 50s)

> Having to work with people who don't understand the job, don't know what the fuck they're doing and they think they know the job better than me. (male, 20s)

> I have worked in a warehouse that delivered tax-free wares to ships… The job was very physical, monotonous, boring, without any interesting or exciting aspects at all. (male, 20s)

> For a period I worked for a temp agency, trying several different kinds of work. One of the problems was that I asked too many questions. I wanted to know the exact kind of work, the working hours, the wage, the location, who to contact, could I bring my own food, etc. For me it was just a matter of being properly informed. But the agency was more used to workers just saying 'yes' or 'no' to the jobs they offered and they thought all my asking showed a lack of enthusiasm. (male, 20s)

> Mornings are difficult as I am quite nocturnal. I need structure as to what I would be expected to achieve but I need independence in the direction I want to take to get there. (female, 20s)

I worked in a bead workshop… I liked working there but sometimes found it a little boring and repetitive. (male, 40s)

Contracts manager for a repair company. Fine when left to 'get on with it' but too constrained when in [an] office with others looking over my shoulder. Also too many things to deal with at once – unable to deal with any single issues comprehensively. Everything seemed to be a fudged solution. (male, 40s)

One thing that does give me cause for worry is losing a client and having to find new ones, that isn't good for me. It takes me two or three hours (or even days) thinking about things before I'm ready to pick up the phone and call people out of the blue. (male, 40s)

I currently work as a healthcare assistant in a large hospital. This is a constant source of difficulty, but I get by with medication, support from a psychiatrist and the knowledge that there is not much else that I can do. I don't have many skills, and given my difficulties, am just relieved to be holding down a job and living independently. It is an over-stimulated, stressful, high workload job wherein my job description seems to change without warning. Quite how long I will cope with this is something I am not sure of. It's been six months, and I am increasingly unhappy with it and the immense stress that it puts on me. (female, 20s)

I had a profound inability to mingle and do the social thing. I am not able to manage situations that are not defined and rehearsed, where I might be expected to be spontaneous and/or come up with interesting things to say to people at random. This was the case for the whole of my work life. (male, 60s)

I misunderstand people's intentions at work. A week ago my boss showed me something. I said it was nice and walked away. Everyone laughed and I turned around to find out that he hadn't actually been showing it to me; he wanted me to do something specific with it. This information was, apparently, conveyed within and by his facial gestures; gestures that I had not picked up on and hadn't recognised. Mistakes like this are an everyday occurrence and I often go home exhausted or crying as a result of the sheer effort it takes me to survive the interaction. (female, 20s)

The amount of people, the high levels of interaction required, the lights, the fast pace that leaves me no time to process and decode things I don't understand, the fine motor skills that are required for various bits of my job, the need for team work and communication. As I write this, I am increasingly despondent by the lack of fit, and of my seeming lack of alternatives. I overcome what I do because of a determination not to be beaten, and by a determination to live as close to a normal life as possible. I will try and try again. Yesterday will not necessarily repeat itself today (it usually does, but I try not to let that put me off). (female, 20s)

The entire place was one massive mix of politics and infighting which I just couldn't comprehend and work my way round. I'm still not sure how I could have done better without turning into a total bastard like the boss, which isn't my style. (male, 40s)

I worked in a company importing and exporting technical manuals to the Middle East. This was a job with tight deadlines, where ever-changing demands and instructions were the norm, and where I didn't receive the training necessary to fulfil my role competently. (male, 40s)

My job involves a lot of social entertaining, team events, large parties, noisy events, and I often find myself drifting to the edge and melting away, feeling very tired/drained. (male, 40s)

People who tell me I am wrong when I know I'm right. (male, 20s)

One person at work who also had [a] drink problem, starting buying me alcohol at the end of [the] night shift – parcels at boot of my car. I knew more than him intellectually and in the job. Led me astray. Started major drink problem. (male, 20s)

Salesman for a courier service (lasted only for a few weeks). Having to make small talk and sell to strangers. Having to be sociable. (male, 30s)

Have done bar work. Manager had a go at me for not being sociable. Worked at [convenience store]. Had to stack shelves with non-existent stock. Didn't train me. Assumed I could do things I wasn't shown how to do. Fired me. (male, 20s)

I've been fired from every job I've had so far. In my first job, it was because they changed the deal on me. I said I wouldn't do sales, and they agreed. Later when things got tough, they wanted me to go up to people and sell stuff to them. When I failed to do it to their satisfaction, they fired me... My fifth job was the worst. My boss was always hovering near me, checking to make sure I did no wrong... He fired me when I refused to sign a new contract that severely limited my rights, for less compensation. (male, 30s)

My present job as security supervisor at the airport involves dealing with people who do not appreciate my contribution, which they perceive as an annoyance, although the end result is for their own benefit. I find this irritating as I do most things where narrow-minded people are incapable of seeing the broader picture, concentrating on their own selfish and foolish immediate needs. (male, 50s)

During my training as a middle-school teacher I discovered that the large-group setting of a classroom was very unsuitable for me. (male, 60s)

Phone calls, especially to outside places, that makes me hold my breath because I could not predict what was going to happen next and I lose my 'script' of what I am going to say and how to say that in a way that I don't lose my way. Having a script is absolutely essential until I am comfortable with all of the possible responses from the mystery person on the other end of the call. (male, 30s)

I took up this job [call-centre agent] at the age of 60, having left academic contract work. The demands were horrendous – constant pressure of incoming calls, constant adaptation to new enquiries and personalities, a very buzzy and unreflective work environment, the need to handle social interaction (on the phone) at the same time as doing data manipulation on-screen and strategy (figuring out what to do with the caller). I coped bravely – and in fact, quite well – with the three-month initial period but my ability to sustain this broke down within the fourth month. I went on sick leave and resigned after six months, with a breakdown. (male, 60s)

I worked in a supermarket for a while when young, it was sensorily overloading. My work ethic (fair day's pay for a fair day's work) and inability to accept failure overrode my desire for decent financial reward and discomfort of the environment. (male, 30s)

I like to make sure I have all equipment, paperwork, tools for the whole day ready before I start. When a management person changes their mind this causes me stress. Too many chiefs, not enough Indians. (male, 20s)

I do not suffer fools gladly, especially when they should know better. I have often been better than my managers and this has caused problems. (male, 70s)

Sometimes it's very frustrating as I often don't understand why other people are considered to be more part of the team than me. (male, 30s)

Travelling to and from work

The necessity to travel to get to one's job is a fact of life for the majority of people and requires an ability that is often overlooked or not given enough consideration when supporting those with AS into work. I have known several people who would feel incapable of getting on a bus if it was too crowded and others who become highly anxious if a planned bus didn't arrive and they had to find an alternative route. I was told of an AS charity that organised a day trip and hired a coach large enough for each person to have their own double seat, so that no one would have to sit next to anyone else. If a person is physically unable to get to work, their options for employment may be limited to the distance they can realistically walk from their home. For many reasons, public transport is often very stressful for them to tolerate. A few of these are:

- sensory issues of close physical contact with others, as well as smells, noise and temperature
- social interaction required with driver/conductor
- understanding timetables
- knowing routes
- delays and diversions requiring new route or alternative travel plans which may not be known
- late arrival of bus/train meaning late arrival at work.

Allowing some degree of flexibility in start and finish times would alleviate the problem of rush hour crowds. Wearing headphones or earplugs, listening to music, can block out unwanted noise and overload in busy places and sunglasses can help to limit brightness or glare. Walking or travelling by bicycle not only avoids the close physical contact of public transport but also provides exercise, which relaxes and stimulates the production of endorphins, which enhance positive moods and alleviate depression. Alternatively, many people could work at home for some or all of their work hours. A person with AS is likely to be far more productive in the stress-free environment of their own home, than in a social environment that requires an ordeal by bus to get there. People with AS are often very conscientious and honest and could be trusted entirely to work for the period required unsupervised. The answers below reveal that transport is an issue for many, but a sanctuary for a few. Some have devised their own strategies for dealing with the potential stress and sensory issues by finding work very close to home, only travelling at certain times or changing transport methods:

> Unless I stick to the same routes to work I can easily get disorientated or lost. I stick to the ways that I know. (male, 50s)

> I dislike very much taking the bus to work. In the morning, when it's cool and not so many people are on the bus, then it is okay. But in the afternoon, when I go home, it is a nightmare for me. It is often very hot inside the bus, it is crowded and noisy, and it takes ages for the bus to get anywhere because of traffic. The time it takes for me to go from having a nice and pleasant day, to be exhausted, on the verge of panic, sweating heavily, and unable to do much of anything for the rest of the day, is precisely the time it takes for the bus to go from downtown and to the stop where I get off. (male, 20s)

> I become extremely frustrated if I am made later by traffic conditions (not rare on a 45 mile commute) rather than by my own design. I invariably arrive at work 30 to 40 minutes early, but this is not an infallible solution! (male, 40s)

> Dislike of tubes and trains. Crowded, hot and smelly. Cycle to work every day. Physical exercise also has a calming effect. (male, 40s)

> One of my clients has offices right in the middle of London. I work round that by either going into town stupidly early, taking the 6.30 train if I have to be there at the start of play, or waiting until 9.30 and getting in later. Then I stay until 8 in the evening so I can get a more relaxed journey back. Sometimes I walk from the train station to the office, depending on the state of the tube system. I usually let three or four go past and choose one I get into comfortably or head out and walk. I have waited anything up to half an hour before giving up and getting out of the station. (male, 40s)

I absolutely hate getting on the bus. Until I get my driving licence back (drink-driving offence and epilepsy), I have to go by bus. I live in the country so I have no choice to get bus to work. School kids on bus freak me out – they chatter and natter. Claustrophobia – I don't have control over it, forced in a tin box. Know you have to be on it until you get to your destination. No control. (male, 20s)

I prefer not to travel to/from work, but it's a necessity. I can handle the bus/train because I've been doing it all my life. I just fold into my own universe and shut everything out. I also have a PSP [hand-held games console], which helps a lot. I've hacked it up so that it's also a book reader, so I can read on the train as well. I keep a digital library of about 50,000 books on my computer and copy whatever I'm interested in at the time to the PSP. Lately, I've been learning microeconomic and macroeconomic theory, and have learned all about the global banking scam called fractional reserve banking. (male, 30s)

I actually like the travelling to and from work. There is the calmness that comes from that. The transitioning from work to home that comes from travelling to or from work has a calming effect on me. The bus/underground is a good thing because I know that while I am on it, there is just a good deal of time to unwind after a strange day at the office. (male, 30s)

I fly a lot on business and desperately stick to my preferred airline to give me control, reduce stress, and preferred status gives me priority security queue, lounge access, etc. – helping to reduce stress. (male, 40s)

Socialising at work

There is sometimes the misconception that work is about the actual task that you are employed and paid to do and that your skill in carrying out this task is all that stands between you and success. This is rarely the case. The workplace is a social environment above all else. In many cases, you will spend more hours of your life with your work colleagues than with any other human being. You didn't choose them and you can't change them unless one of you changes jobs. Work can be a minefield of unspoken rules and changing allegiances. Get it wrong and offend someone, and going to work can be a misery. There are similarities with the school playground, which was another area that people with AS often found stressful and confusing. Bullying can be commonplace at work as well as school, and those with AS can find themselves either a target or excluded for the same reasons as when they were a child: obvious lack of understanding of the infinite and ever-changing hidden social curriculum, being clever and too good at the job, awkwardness, refusal or inability to make flexible small talk. (Bullying is looked at in Chapter 4 (see pp.90–94).) Like it or not, distancing yourself from the social fray may give you the reputation of being aloof or antisocial. If you are not concerned what others think of you and prefer to continue as you are, that is fine, but it is good to know the possible consequences of your actions, so that you can make an informed choice. It is fair to assume that most people have no idea how stressful and tiring negotiating conversations and social interactions is for someone with AS, and that they would probably be kinder and more patient if they did. Finding someone you can trust to translate the banter and expectations would be helpful. Even something as simple as not offering to make tea or coffee for colleagues, when this is the norm in your workplace, can leave you isolated and viewed as antisocial. These small social niceties are highly valued by many people without AS and may make the difference to whether you are promoted, given a pay rise, or remain doing the same dull tasks year in, year out, as succinctly put by one person with AS:

> Your social acceptance in the workplace can be a more significant factor in your progression through the ranks than your ability to do the job required of you. (male, 40s)

This is entirely unfair, but unfortunately that is the way it is, and learning the non-AS social language in order to get where you want to be may be the only route. Relationships are very important in most workplaces – it can be much like school and the same characters will be there.

Watching what other people do is a useful exercise, so that you can work out the level of interaction and reciprocity and join in at the appropriate level. Offer to make the coffee – even if you don't want to and can't see the point. It will go a long way to being 'one of the team' (if that's what you want to be). Do what you can for others and they will reciprocate – it's how the (social) world goes round. For an employer, it is important that you are aware of the difficulties that a person with AS may be having with the general banter of the workplace. They may need some help in interpreting what is being said and in putting it in perspective. They may struggle to differentiate between good-humoured teasing and offensive remarks and may find a noisy, talkative environment impossible to work in. Lunch times and breaks can be a minefield for those with AS – much like the playground at school – a setting with no structure and without the focus on the work. Work may be the only topic that the person with AS has to talk about, when others may prefer to discuss personal matters, holidays and the like. Listening to the type of conversations and topics discussed can help provide clues as to appropriate subjects to ask questions about. People need to believe that you are genuinely interested in their answers to want to engage in conversation.

> Sometimes I can get involved in office gossip, but mainly listening. (male, 40s)

> I get told off for farting loudly at work. When I asked a colleague whether everyone else farted as much as I do but simply does it quietly, he refused to engage in the conversation and told me to find something worth worrying about. I wasn't worried; I was genuinely interested in knowing. (male, 30s)

> It differs from day to day. Sometimes I talk with my colleagues a great deal. Other days I'm not in the mood and just concentrate on my work. (male, 30s)

> I find them [social relationships] difficult, but they work best when people are clear and explicit in what they say. Also when the amount of time is limited so that I can bow out gracefully when overloaded. (male, 30s)

> I tend to spend my breaks privately in the public canteen. This negates the need for small talk with colleagues (which I

am very poor at) and also avoids the possibility of boring them to embarrassment with work issues (which I am very good at!). (male, 40s)

I have tried, a few times, to go to lunch with other people. This hasn't worked for three reasons:

1. The lighting in the canteen was horrendous and gave me a headache.
2. I could not make conversation and felt overwhelmed.
3. The food was not to my liking.

I choose instead to go home for lunch and take the few minutes alone to recover from the stress of the morning and find the determination to go back for the afternoon. I often need to cry a little bit. (female, 20s)

I always spend my lunchtimes on my own, reading newspapers and speaking to nobody if I can help it. This enables me to process what I have experienced and to prepare for the afternoon. Since giving up alcohol, I rarely socialise with work colleagues immediately after work, I prefer to go home and spend time on my own in my room. (male, 40s)

I can talk to people quite happily, but on my own terms – when I want to. If someone is too cheery and I am in a shitty mood, I will just walk away from them. (male, 20s)

We have lots of social events at work. I avoid them whenever possible. Everyone knows my name, but I find it nearly impossible to remember theirs. It makes talking more awkward than normal. I never have anything to talk about besides projects at work, or interesting theories I'm working on, and nobody is really interested in that. (male, 40s)

I find it irritating having to listen to 'small talk' (usually of a complaining and whining nature) indulged in by other employees who seem more interested in belittling the job than getting on with doing it. (male, 30s)

I have never liked work social events, Xmas parties, etc., as I always felt like an outcast. I always used my birthday being close to Xmas as an excuse to avoid. I have also tended not to organise drinks at work for my birthday. (male, 40s)

Generally, I struggle with in-office friendly banter, and as a result have always tended to distance myself from people, often becoming friends only after I or they move on (if then). Tend to skip the niceties and just jump in with my work focus discussion. (male, 40s)

Every so often I dig myself into a hole, speaking my mind on stuff and/or upsetting people, usually on email. I am often worried about whether people accept my perspective. Sometimes my frustrations leak out in some form of anger management issues – going on a rant about something or other. (male, 40s)

Office politics is the one thing about work that makes me the most angry and clueless. There is little that can be done about it as I am more worried about the work than about other people's whims. It bothers me when other people's issues stop work or disrupt work in such a way as to confuse me or stop me from working. (male, 40s)

Physical and sensory environment

Unless you are fortunate to work at home or in an environment of your choosing, it is likely that you will have little control over where you are expected to carry out your work. In an office environment, this may involve flickering, humming lighting, temperature set at a level not of your liking, noise from other people and the outside world (passing traffic, etc.), distractions and many other potentially uncomfortable sensory disturbances. Many non-AS people do not have the finely tuned sensory abilities of those with AS and may find it hard to believe that the low buzz of a phone charger can cause such discomfort, or that trying to work in an open plan office is a near impossibility. The person with AS may be seen as 'making a fuss' or being unreasonable. There is plenty of written evidence to demonstrate the validity of requests for environmental adjustments, which must be supported under disability law (in the UK). For an employer, it's important to understand that the provision of a desk lamp, or allowing the wearing of headphones in a noisy office, can make the difference between employment and unemployment for someone with AS. Environmental sensory sensitivity is often cited as the most significant aspect of AS difficulties. Noise and lights seem to be the main culprits here:

> Flickering lights really drive me crazy unless I am totally focused on analysis or there is a critical situation I am managing. (male, 50s)

> Only the people. I wear headphones and listen to music to try to block out their unwanted drone and din. (male, 30s)

> Understanding of AS has helped me to recognise these and also to deal with them by facing up to them. For example, chairs scraping on tiled floors is excruciatingly painful but 'that's just the AS', as is the smell of cleaning fluids on the carpets that makes me feel physically sick. (male, 40s)

> I don't like people looking over my shoulder, so I prefer to have my back towards a wall. I have discomfort with too much light as well, so I don't want to be near a window without heavy curtains or blinds. Too much noise and movement around me tends to distract me a lot as well. I don't mind people around me talking, but I prefer conversations to be lowered. Motion attracts my eyes almost instantly, so people sitting nervously on their chairs or walking a lot around me simply exhausts me. (male, 20s)

> There are lots of noises that I can't cope with. People moving one piece of paper over another or touching their skin makes sounds I don't like. I can't cope with polystyrene. I block my ears or run away. For me there is some kind of connection between touch and sound. They cross over a bit. (female, 20s)

When colleagues come too close and touch my arm or slap me on the back, feel 'you have invaded my bubble, my space, my environment' and no one can invade it unless I invite them in. (male, 20s)

In my home office I tend to live a bit like a hermit in semi-darkness most of the time with a couple of spotlights lighting up the desk area. I do like to have music playing but I can switch it off instantly if I need to concentrate on anything or talk on the phone, but when it's going I probably have it quite loud, otherwise I tend to get very sleepy. (male, 40s)

Certain lighting, especially when tired, gives a bad taste and smell – signs of the beginnings of an epileptic fit. Physically cover my eyes to shut out light. (male, 20s)

Certain noises make me cry – pitch and frequency. Lower noise – laptop just being on (low hum of fan) really annoying. Higher frequency. (male, 20s)

Can't stop self listening in on everything going on. Can't tune sound out. If the light is the wrong colour I get very annoyed. Would focus on monitor to ignore it. Keep seeing patterns. e.g. (the) way things are laid out. Can't stop looking at them. (male, 40s)

Sometimes the smell of the house when the home owners are from the Middle East or India, I have to breathe through my mouth and go out to my truck several times for fresh air. (male, 30s)

I tend to work from home as I find open plan offices impossible to work in. I cannot cut out background conversations at all. Always hear what others are saying and then end up interrupting to make comments, which sometimes is of course considered irritating to others. (male, 40s)

When there are sudden noises and work/files that should be where I parked them last but are not there. That will cause me to jump out sometimes and look at things that would give me cause to be worried (electrical outlets, etc.). (male, 30s)

Dealing with stress

For most people, there will come a time when things become difficult at work, either because of the workload, relationships with colleagues or other stress of some kind. For people with AS, this level of stress can be a daily occurrence, causing high levels of anxiety and physical and mental strain. This may be caused by added sensory stress, as discussed above. The main coping strategy for managing stress at work appears to be either absenteeism or leaving the job. This is not recommended as it can lead to dismissal and rarely prevents the same problem arising at a later date. The communication difficulties implicit in AS may make the problem bigger: the person may be less able to discuss their feelings and concerns at an early stage to prevent the stress becoming unmanageable. Also, with a more limited social network at work and outside, the person may have no one to offload to, or discuss issues with before they become too big to manage. The all-or-nothing AS thinking can fail to see possible solutions other than just leaving the job to escape the stress. Without anyone to share alternative perspectives, this may be seen as the only viable option. There is also a tendency for some with AS to find it difficult to accept help and admit 'failure' (as they see it) and so they will say nothing. A more dangerous, and possibly common, strategy is to block out the stress with alcohol or drugs. Five people (out of 25) reported drinking 'too much' on a regular basis in order to combat stress:

> I have given up full-time employment as a result of stress leading to alcohol addiction. I now work part time in a relaxed environment, and find that this is a lifestyle I can easily manage... I have used alcohol and tranquilisers to enable me to function in a stressful environment. (male, 40s)

> Difficulty in taking responsibility for things at home due to obsessive preoccupation with work. When at home 'the lights are on but no one is there' was a common remark from family. I have not had a sick day in 15 years. (male, 50s)

The job that I had before I went to university was one that I hated. I drank too much, occasionally self-harmed (although this was very occasional), had four months off sick in one block and regular little periods of sick leave. Eventually I left. I don't do any of these things anymore, but I cry more. This isn't depression, it's a transitory outlet. (female, 20s)

The pressure of deadlines for marking, classroom observations, or delivering a poor lesson invariably lead to further isolation from my family as I tend to concentrate on work even more in an attempt to address the problems. I have been known on very rare occasions to contract deadly 'man-flu' when things become too overbearing! (male, 40s)

Both in my working life and school life, stress makes me stay at home, resulting in high levels of absence, which isn't tolerated for very long. This is the absolutely most defining feature of me when I'm stressed. If I'm stressed, I am unable to make anything work really. I can't make any decisions or take initiative to get anything done. (male, 20s)

I do probably drink way too much. It's sometimes the only way I can get to sleep because I have so many thoughts about everything running through my head, so I tend to turn the phones off after about 19.00 unless I know I have a call booked. If I'm working I don't drink even if it's offered and never if I'm driving either, I know if I have one it won't stop there so I don't do it at all. (male, 40s)

I find company politics drives me mad, and indeed I managed to make myself redundant on one occasion because I could not suppress my views on the mistakes I felt we were making. As a result of travel, bad diet and shutting myself away I became somewhat overweight, and then last year when I became isolated after the company acquisition I lost 1.5 stone in about six to nine months. (male, 40s)

I have sometimes become introspective and concentrated on my work. I did have a breakdown when the stress of teaching in a sink school got me down. (male, 60s)

My wife says that sometimes I bring the stress home with me and treat her and the rest of the family like dirt and I have a very short fuse. (male, 30s)

Meltdowns can and do create absenteeism. Stress meltdowns, overwhelm meltdowns create issues that are difficult to overcome. (male, 30s)

If I get too stressed, I take a sick day and stay home. Sometimes I'll just telecommute instead of coming in. (male, 30s)

Anger at co-workers gets suppressed in order for work to get done. Taking a walk to regroup sometimes gets necessary when major disruptions do happen and I have difficulties. (male, 40s)

I have occasional days off with stress and this is virtually inevitable, but generally only about half a dozen days per annum… In my last job, after doing fine under one director, a new one arrived and she was a bully and I was off sick a lot and ended up being sacked. (male, 50s)

Stress-related illness: exhaustion, signed off sick for more than a month, resignation (three times), breakdowns (four times). Tempered by 'working at home', not actually doing a full day's work and not meeting all the expectations of the job role. More recently, prescribed anti-depressants (for anxiety). Never resorted to alcohol. The solution has always been 'space', freed from the incomprehensible and relentless social demands that emanate facelessly from 'out there'. (male, 60s)

I nearly killed myself working too hard trying to do my old job and new job at the same time, not feeling I could call for support, and only extreme pressure led me to ask. (male, 40s)

> I have a mechanism for coping with stressful situations at work. In my mind, I isolate the situation from the other events going on, I then deal with the stressful situation on its own merits, keeping in mind that no matter how bad this is it is only an individual situation and does not need to adversely affect the rest of my working day. (male, 50s)

Avoidance of stress and simply coping with the differences that AS brings, particularly in social interaction, marks work as a place of potential anxiety. The comments here are mostly negative, but show a great amount of awareness about these situations that have occurred. Most of the individuals remain in work despite these difficulties, and express a continued desire to do so. This self-awareness can be helpful in reflecting on how a situation can be avoided in the future.

Communicating difficulties to a manager or colleague is important. This does not need to be spoken verbally initially, if expressing yourself is difficult. Write a letter or email explaining what problems you are having, why you are unable to speak directly about them and what support you would like (if you know). Others may have no idea that you are struggling or having problems and will not know unless you tell them. If they do not know, they will be unable to do anything to alleviate your stress or difficulties. Rather than dealing with stress when it arises, it would be preferable to establish a work environment which does not cause high levels of stress. Prevention is much more manageable, but requires a knowledge of what is required to keep stress levels low and performance levels high and the willingness to communicate this to others. Unfortunately, that is exactly what didn't happen in the following case study.

Case study: a tale of unsuccessful employment

The following case study is taken from interviews carried out by Didier Montillaud, a volunteer mentor with ASpire, and reports on an employment situation. The perspective of employer (Patrick), employee (Simon) and mentor (Didier) are provided to highlight how, despite best intentions on the part of all concerned, sometimes things don't work out as planned. It also illustrates the point that support is required for so many people and that, without it, jobs can be lost due to avoidable circumstances.

Names and any identifying features have been changed where necessary. This situation is likely to be typical of many, where education, awareness and communication support come too late to prevent the person from losing their job. Didier did not become involved in this situation until later as the person he was supporting, Simon, did not make him aware at an earlier stage that there was a problem. Simon wanted to deal with it on his own and only asked for help when the situation had become unmanageable for him.

Patrick's story: the employer

The workplace in question is a food shop that also sells sandwiches, hot drinks and snacks which are reheated in a microwave oven on the premises. Staff working there operate the tills, prepare sandwiches and other snacks, keep shelves filled with goods and carry out other tasks as required.

The shop was newly opened. While the owners were setting up their new business, they also needed to recruit staff. They went to the local Jobcentre and there they were able to make contact with a government appointed, supported employment scheme for people with disabilities. The organisation helped Patrick to set up interviews for new staff. Simon was one of the interviewees. Patrick recalls that he came across as one of the better candidates. His CV, albeit somewhat inflated, looked impressive for the kind of responsibilities and experience he was recruiting to. Patrick says that he expects candidates to inflate their CV: 'This is the done thing in any industry; everyone wants to make themselves look good.'

All staff were employed full time. Soon after opening the shop, the owners realised that they had employed too many staff for the needs of the business, so they unfortunately had to reduce their numbers by giving notice to those with lesser abilities and commitment to the job. Simon was retained because he was one of the best members of staff at that point. There were further reductions in staff numbers at a later date, but Simon was still meeting Patrick's expectations, so he stayed on past a second wave of staff losses.

The work was arranged in two shift patterns; one commencing at 7am and ending at 2pm or 3pm, with the second running from 2pm until 8pm. Simon was always on time for any of the shifts he was scheduled to work on. He was enthusiastic, hard-working, compliant, and produced good results in acceptable timescales. The owners noticed that he was good in the kitchen, so they often gave him the responsibility of preparing the sandwiches and other snacks. Simon was efficient, quick, and maintained his enthusiasm. He understood the functions of the complex pricing machine sooner than Patrick, and in fact showed his manager how it worked. He also managed to work out how to remove parts of the oven doors to clean them better, which he was also able to explain to Patrick.

For a while Simon was thriving at work and Patrick states how happy he was with his work, but then things began to change:

> It took us a while to work out what was going on. Simon would come to work as usual, carry out his tasks as required, work fast and find himself with spare time on his scheduled activities. This would not be a problem because we were then able to make use of him on the shop floor. However, slowly, Simon was not to be found after he had finished his tasks in the kitchen. He used to spend time in the toilet or outside at the back of the shop.

If either the owners or any of his colleagues were looking for him they would not be able to locate him in the shop.

His behaviour at work continued to worsen. He used to set up a 'scene' in the kitchen, such as leaving the oven door open as if to indicate that he was hard at work baking and setting the kitchen to look as if other activities were taking place, whereas he was in the toilet or hiding at the back of the shop. They began to realise that he wasn't able to sustain a full day's work:

> If he arrived for a morning shift he was perfect until about midday. After that his energies had run out and he was unable to communicate reasonably with us, let alone engage with any other tasks we would ask him to carry out.

Patrick describes Simon as occasionally becoming challenging and difficult to manage. His colleagues too began to find him difficult to get on
with. He would use the internet facilities on the tills and surf for hours,
even though he had been expressly asked not to do this. This pattern
went on for a while: 'We couldn't fathom any of the reasons for his behaviour.'

Patrick felt that they tried to support him in any way they could. They
liked him as a person and valued him as a member of staff. He was
meeting all their expectations and his flow of energy and the quality of
his work hadn't diminished. However, when he reached his limits he
would immediately stop producing any work and his behaviour would
become problematic for the managers and his colleagues.

> I used to be rather direct and uncompromising in my
> instructions. This would work for a very short while. Simon
> wasn't able to motivate himself. He had no energy left
> anyway, so he would drift and again disappear. We would
> have to be on his back incessantly to make sure we'd get
> some work out of him for the rest of his shift. He had by now
> been employed by us for about six weeks and we felt that we
> had tried all we could to support him and motivate him, but
> we needed to run a business and we had now come to the
> decision that we couldn't continue to employ him. So we
> gave him notice. Surprisingly some of our staff, although
> they had been antagonised by him, reacted to our decision
> and pleaded in his defence to make us rethink our decision
> to dismiss him.

At that point Didier became involved, as Simon had told him that he
had been fired and had asked for help with the situation. Didier
spoke to Patrick and explained that Simon had AS, which explained
the reasons for his behaviour. He offered to give Patrick the support
to enable Simon to rebuild his credibility and remain employed.
Patrick accepted willingly and felt relieved, finally, that someone had
enlightened him. He had had no information from either Simon or the
employment service about AS.

A programme of support was discussed with Simon present. There
would be a three-way weekly review meeting with Simon, Patrick and

Didier to iron out difficulties and Didier would be at the end of a phone as and when needed. All appeared to be going well.

Didier then went on holidays for two weeks, and on his return tried to call Simon to agree the next meeting with Patrick. It took some time for Simon to return his calls, but he eventually agreed a date to meet. He didn't show up on the day of the arranged meeting. On calling Patrick, Didier was told that Simon had deteriorated since the workplace meeting and that he had just worked his last shift. Patrick says with some regret about the situation:

> Had I known that Simon had AS at the start of his employment, although I knew nothing about AS, I would have tried to provide a more focused support. I realised that Simon wasn't able to work a full day, but I had employed him full time. I think that if I had known that he had such problems, I would have discussed this with him and I might have offered to employ him part time. In the circumstances, I didn't know what to do other than continue to make clear my expectations of his fulfilling a full day's work for me, because that was the agreement we had at the start and he never came forward to ask for any special treatment.
>
> I think Simon has limited energy. He uses it very quickly because he works fast at anything he does and doesn't pace himself. Even if he slowed down, he might not be able to sustain more than four to five hours of any activity per day. He loses interest in what he does rather quickly. I think that once he's used up his energy for one thing, his attention or motivation has also been used up for anything else. So he then drifts and goes into his Asperger world where no one can reach him. He would be best suited to work of no more than five hours at anything he takes on. In the end we were exasperated and exhausted by his behaviour and his storytelling in an attempt to mask his disability, so we let him go.

Didier's story: the mentor

Didier provides mentor support for Simon through ASpire, an adult AS mentoring project, and has been working with him for over a year on a variety of targets and issues. Some background on Simon and his life up to this point is included here to provide a fuller picture of him. This is collated from interviews with Simon carried out by Didier.

Simon is 23 years of age. Simon's parents divorced before he was 10 years of age and he and his younger brother then lived with their mother. His father attended reputable universities and acquired good qualifications. His whole family is rather academic and seems to prize intellectual achievements. Simon's father lives and works in Asia, where he teaches. His brother has qualified from university too and has travelled the world, and his grandfather was a famous writer. Simon wishes to match his family's academic achievements.

He was diagnosed with AS at the age of 16, in his last year of secondary school. He had spent many years in trouble both at school and at home before his diagnosis. He was initially seen as disruptive by the school system and this continued for some years before his mother managed to secure his diagnosis. As a result, his education suffered as well as his relationship with his family, particularly his mother and brother; his grandmother appears to be the one person in the family system with whom Simon has managed to construct a reasonably trusting and rewarding relationship.

Currently, Simon lives in a shared house. His mother lives overseas but has returned to the UK to support Simon for up to one year, when she will leave again. His father still lives overseas and only his grandmother remains living locally to him.

Simon will soon be evicted from his current accommodation for irregular payment of rent and because of his general behaviour, which has antagonised his co-tenants and his landlord. He receives quite a lot of help from his mother, both emotionally and financially. She has paid several deposits to enable him to access housing with private landlords. He lived with his mother until his teens but became unruly and occasionally 'physical' with her. She eventually registered him homeless as she was unable to continue managing him at home. Due to his diagnosis, Simon was soon housed by a housing association. Initially all was well, but then his behaviour became problematic for his co-tenants. He used to play interactive computer games in his room and interact with the various characters in the story by shouting. His interaction with his co-tenants was difficult, owing to his inability to relate in a socially appropriate manner. He then inherited a large sum of money, which precluded him from continuing to benefit from public housing or any other type of welfare benefits. He was evicted from his home for that reason, as well as for his behaviour.

Within a year of receiving his inheritance, Simon had spent it all and had even begun to have financial difficulties. He requested support from ASpire and began receiving mentoring support at that point in his life. The role of the mentor is sometimes to model ways of relating to the world, in general, which are supposed to demonstrate appropriate, responsible, worthwhile behaviour and responses in social situations. This can be very helpful to someone with AS who has few peers to learn from. The principles of 'social' mentoring aim to enable the person to learn and then hopefully emulate some of those behaviours and responses, thus maximising their options to build up their socialisation skills, as well as reducing social isolation and teaching strategies for coping with life in general.

During his mentoring meetings, Simon demonstrates a surprising ability to interact appropriately. He presents himself as confident, capable and achieving, and discusses his academic and professional ambitions. He makes every effort he can to behave as 'normal' as possible, and can be convincing enough. However, Simon is a tall-story teller of epic dimensions: there have been reports of jobs interviews or jobs, which he has talked about for several weeks, providing detailed anecdotes about them, before finally admitting to having entirely fabricated the story. This has continued with tales about some of his academic activities (not having signed up for, or attended courses he mentioned), including details of his achievements, until once again he is unable to pretend any longer and has to admit to another fabrication.

Simon usually doesn't like talking about anything too serious. He is quick to postpone an action, thus regularly putting off any possibility of making inroads with any aspects of his life that require attention and practical application to achieve results; progress is very slow.

Simon is quite depressed and spends long hours playing with his computer at home. He sees the one trusted friend he has – a school friend

– when he has got money to go out, but of late these occasions are few and far between. His lack of trust in others, as well as his lack of life experience, compounds his low self-esteem and his ability to engage with the world and the people in it. He also has a poor track record of managing money. He is currently in a lot of debt and regularly avoids dealing with practical issues involving his money. He usually ignores his post for several days, weeks or months, with some bank correspondence not having been opened two years on. When he manages to open his post he still won't deal with it, unless it is from an official source and he is required to attend an appointment. Simon forgot to inform the appropriate government department of his change of address and consequently lost part of his welfare benefits last year. This has further aggravated his already disastrous financial situation.

Lately Simon has agreed to review his situation and look at ways of improving some of his personal issues. He thinks he would benefit from personal therapy, but he is also considering family therapy. There are many well-intentioned beginnings, cancelled by retractions at the last moment or stalling type behaviours, which indicate that getting nearer, let alone achieving, any planned action is still anxiety-provoking. He is able to assess what his difficulties are – for instance, how he should manage his finances appropriately. However, he struggles to imagine how he could change his fundamental behaviour to improve those aspects of his life, which remain problematic and continue to prevent him from living a fuller, socially involved life.

Progress continues to be slow, but recently Simon has, with his mentor and mother, created an action plan which aims to enable him to address his continuing difficulties.

Simon will continue to receive support from a mentor for as long as he finds the process valuable and continues to engage in it. This is the background from which Simon began work for the employer mentioned above. Now he gives his side of the story.

Simon's story: the employee

I was employed in August 07 in a food retail shop. The job was arranged via [name of employment support scheme]. I had been referred there since I had been unemployed/

signing on for more than six months at the Jobcentre. The employment scheme takes over the Jobcentre's responsibilities and acts as an employment agency. They have helped me better than the Jobcentre, who never managed to find me any jobs to apply to. Initially I didn't want to work full time because I knew I couldn't sustain full time work. However [the employment scheme] managed to convince me that it was a good opportunity and that I should go for it. The arrangements are that the interviews they line up are compulsory. That interview was recorded on their systems, so they intimated that my only option, if I really didn't want to take that full time post, would be to mess up during the interview. They would have then sent me for other interviews, possibly part-time ones. We discussed my AS, but they suggested I didn't mention it at the interview stage. I could mention it later on. They pointed out that, in the first instance, it was more important that my employer thought of me as employable. So neither they nor I mentioned anything to Patrick. I also didn't mention it to them afterwards because I didn't want to be treated differently and I thought it would prejudice my promotion. I had initially thought of telling them after I successfully completed my probationary period. But then I never got round to telling them. I had been unemployed for a while and I was bored. I was desperate to get a job. I had just returned from holidaying at my mother's house. We had been talking about work, so I also wanted to make her proud of me. I did the best interview I could and I got the job. It was good at the beginning. I was working hard. I was quite pleased to be working. There was the possibility of promotion into management, so I worked hard as I wanted to achieve that. However, it began to fall apart from there on. Since I was working full time, I began to be tired and find it difficult to continue. I was sometimes on the till, but I found it boring being there with not much to do. I didn't have internet connection at home at the time, so I'd surf the net with the tills at work. Patrick was very unhappy about it when he found out and told me not to use the internet. So I stopped using it. Still I was bored behind that till, so I would occasionally go on the floor to refill shelves. Patrick asked me not to do that because I should remain behind the till, since it was my allocated job for that period and tills couldn't be left unattended for security reasons. I then went back using the internet and they warned me against using it again. I then moved to the kitchen where I was posted for all my shifts. I was good at it, but it wasn't that interesting, a bit like factory work. I couldn't do anything different; I was not able to imagine a different sandwich; all items had to be made the same. Some of the food was frozen so I only had to unwrap it, put it on a tray and put it in the oven. I could eat well on the job. I was too bored. I started to tell inappropriate jokes with some of my colleagues. I once snapped a Coke from one of my colleague's hands, threw it in the bin and pushed a healthy drink in her hand, mentioning that Coke would make her fat and that she should better drink healthy juices. She didn't like that. I also broke confidentiality with two of my colleagues who were in league to become managers. I passed a conversation on to them that I had overheard from Patrick. I guess I played them off against each other and I found that fun. Patrick was very unhappy about it, they told me not to do that again. In the end my colleagues didn't want to work with me any longer. I eventually lost my job at the end of September.

As Patrick describes, his expectations of Simon were from the perspective of him being a full-time member of staff. Simon had the awareness to recognise his own limitations, but not the ability to communicate and assert these. He was also given poor advice from his employment adviser in being told to apply for full-time jobs and to tell no one of his AS. These two issues cost Simon his job. If he had disclosed his AS, he might have been able to negotiate fewer hours, and other adjustments. It seems that he was able to perform well up to a point but had no means of communicating when he could no longer cope. Adequate assessment from the employment scheme would have managed the expectations of all parties concerned by identifying potential issues from Simon's past work history, which was very small and had not been successful. Simon had never had a full-time job for any length of time, so it might have been useful to consider why this was the case and whether he was capable of actually keeping one. Awareness and disclosure of AS might have altered the outcome of this situation by preparing the employer for the needs of someone with AS. Unfortunately, this was another 'failure' for Simon, which perhaps could have been avoided.

There are many factors that can influence the chances of success that a person with AS will have at any given job, and the ones listed in this chapter will decrease those chances many-fold. Eliminating as many stressors as possible is a good way to reverse this and increase those chances. Awareness of one's own triggers and particular stress points is vital, as is asking for help when you need it – or even just before you need it. It is really OK to ask for help. No one is perfect or can be expected to be able to cope with and know everything. Not even you!

3

Asperger Syndrome and Employment – What Works and Why

It's not all bad news, despite some of the messages from the previous chapter. Now we have looked at situations which have been difficult, it's time to look at some which have provided successful working environments for people with AS. It is useful to try and identify the specifics of these positive experiences and, in some cases, the skills that the individuals had which supported these. It is not possible to provide a template for the job that is most rewarding and least stressful for someone with AS because, like anyone else, everyone is different, but there are some common characteristics which were frequently mentioned and which may help to provide a checklist of the types of job roles that might better suit someone with AS. Some people were very passionate about their enjoyment of their jobs when involved in these activities, despite the fact that these same jobs brought them stress and difficulty at other times – usually the 'other people' elements. Forty-seven per cent of those questioned who were employed worked and were qualified in IT or engineering, with a further 10 per cent employed in specifically mathematical fields, so it may be that certain fields fit more easily with the systemising AS temperament. It may also be that these types of environments attract other people with differing social abilities and that quality of work is measured more highly than socialising. Environments featuring lots of people, teamwork and constantly shifting work tasks and expectations are less likely to suit the AS personality. These types of jobs rely heavily on flexibility, social interaction and multitasking, which are defined as AS areas of weakness within the diagnostic criteria itself.

As well as looking purely at what aspects of work individuals with AS found manageable, I was also interested in why this group of people went to work and wondered if their motivation to do so was different than other people. I also attempted, perhaps unwisely, to encourage some abstract imagination in the participants by asking them to define their 'perfect job'. Some found this an easy task and were able to provide great detail, while others responded with total disdain to what they perceived to be an impossible or ridiculous question!

Despite the difficulties and stress involved, work is said to be good for health. A Healthcare Professionals' Consensus Statement from the UK government Health Work Wellbeing Initiative (2008) states:

> Work which is appropriate to an individual's knowledge, skills and circumstances and undertaken in a safe, healthy and supportive environment, promotes good physical and mental health, prevents ill health and can play an active part in recovering from illness. Good work also rewards the individual with a greater sense of self-worth and has beneficial effects on social functioning.

Improvements in social functioning can certainly occur purely through the extra practice involved in interacting with more people. For some with AS, work can be detrimental to health, but if these guidelines are followed – 'healthy', 'supportive', 'good' work – the statement above is likely to be true for the majority of people with AS as well.

Key factors in successful work

Key factors mentioned for roles that those with AS enjoyed and thrived in were:

- working alone – this was the most commonly mentioned preferred option
- autonomy – making own decisions
- clearly defined role and responsibility

- intellectual challenge

- being respected for skills

- personal interest in subject matter.

The responses demonstrate a considerable degree of self-awareness and reflection within the participants. It is clear that they have given some internal thought to what it is about themselves or their work situations that allows them to perform well and gives them the most satisfaction. The responses may provide some ideas as to the type of task and environment that may suit someone with AS, although, on reflection, it seems that a job containing all of the above factors would be pretty high on most people's list of ideal jobs. Most people wish to be interested in their work, be respected for their skills, know what is expected of them and have some element of control. Only the lone working may not be a preference for some who enjoy the social aspect of the workplace, and for whom the social contacts made at work become the people that they socialise with during their leisure time. Work is also a very common place for people to meet romantic partners, so perhaps it has its uses after all.

> Working alone and doing analysis is my strong point. Such work gives you a certain power, as information from the analytics is very useful and I can spend long hours doing such research. I run critical situations and get a lot of satisfaction out of this activity as I can go very long periods and do not give up until the outcome is achieved. This is disastrous for my family and I am obsessive about my work. (male, 50s)

> I thrive on working as an individual responsible for my own actions and making my own decisions. Other people are not a problem as long as they keep out of my way. (male, 50s)

> For a long time I found being a long-distance lorry driver fulfilling, though this eventually became too mundane and not challenging enough. (male, 40s)

> I enjoyed jobs with not too much pressure. I worked as a lecturer in adult colleges. I like contact with people in a teaching/pupil dynamic but I don't like and am not good at

mingling socially... I was fine with my students as long as I was in my teaching role and therefore the roles and responsibilities were clearly defined. I was fine with my work colleagues if I were in exactly the same dynamic. (male, 40s)

One of the best jobs I've ever had was working as a government research scientist for a rail company, doing maths research bringing university PhD work into practical applications. People almost expect you to be a bit 'odd' and I was left alone for almost five years just getting on with things that I wanted to do. Was a great job. (male, 40s)

I like what I do now [self-employed IT consultant] (except for the paperwork). I do project work, I'm well respected for my skills and the best bit is I get paid for it. (male, 40s)

I worked unpaid as a cleaner at a cathedral for about one year. I arranged that job myself. I was working less than 16 hours per week. I liked that job even though it was volunteer work only. I worked with one other person. We enjoyed working together. (male, 40s)

I enjoy a job where my contribution is appreciated by the people I am dealing with. I enjoyed working at [name of historical site], where I was working as an individual but providing a useful service to a large number of people. (male, 50s)

Computing work for friends. Could get on with own work with others present. (female, 20s)

I have always worked in specialist bookshops, where I could master the subject of the books I sold and feel safe and confident doing my daily work. (male, 40s)

I chose forestry because I enjoyed the fact that I was on my own. Because of my size, I wasn't hired, because people thought I couldn't cope physically. [I] decided to go into IT so I could be on my own. [I] can talk to myself without annoying other people. (male, 20s)

I fared well working alone, only calling for help when I could not make it work alone, or needing a second set of eyes in ways that goes 'does that make sense?'. (male, 30s)

Working with animals – one-to-one basis. (male, 60s)

Well-defined tasks, with patterns that when they did not meet within defined parameters, then call in others to look at it. (male, 40s)

Jobs where I work alone, driving from job-site to job-site. These jobs were low stress, with very dialogue-specific conversations with homeowners. (male, 30s)

I enjoyed working within the confines of a university. At times it was stressful – not the actual work, but the demands of the academics. (male, 60s)

Most of my career has been successful, in the early days working as a programmer so I could just put my head down and do my part of a project by myself. Later moved into other areas but by then was considered as a subject-matter expert and so rarely had to be the initiator. (male, 40s)

While I have worked as a member of a team, I was often ahead of others and was more successful working on my own. (male, 30s)

I mostly work alone and my boss doesn't bother me. He just wants results, and I can deliver, I also have a place next to the window, so the lights don't bother me much. (male, 30s)

Current and previous job, working in an engineering (software) environment – the work is interesting and is the only thing I want to do, the financial gain is not as important as the satisfaction gained by working in the area I do. I mostly work alone, with only the occasional need to collaborate with others. (male, 30s)

When I graduated I tried my hand at various aspects of planning, but eventually specialised in dealing with planning applications, especially the legal side of this. I now realise this is logical for someone with AS as this work is very structured. (male, 50s)

Quite a lot of time I worked on my own, with materials entirely under my control. It was quite easy to let my line manager's attempts to manage me just run off like water off a duck's back. (male, 60s)

I enjoyed working as a shipping agent, solving other people's problems using my own initiative. (male, 50s)

There was a notable culture of facilitation and empower-ment, which was very comforting and meaningful for me and gave opportunities for learning to facilitate and support others. We all had a great deal of autonomy and a minimum of supervision. Thus I was able to be obsessive about my own perspective, and to work in very small, self-selected collaborations with very able and skilful peers. (male, 60s)

Self-awareness

What are the requirements to ensure a satisfactory and successful experi-ence of work and life? Self-awareness is a good start. Once this ability has been practised and developed, it is much easier to consider what kind of strategies may help you to overcome anxieties and difficulties. This can also help you to recognise environments that will best support your skills, as well as those which are best avoided. Some of those questioned showed their own growing reflection on their lives, and the impact they have on others. The following comment is such an example:

Now that I am aware of AS I am thinking very carefully about what sorts of events I can cope with and what events are harder, and trying hard to attend more events despite the difficulty, and organise events in a format I find easier. I also try to make a point of organising one-on-one drinks/lunch so I can build relationships with people. (male, 40s)

Understanding your own self, condition and limitations is a good place to start when deciding what work to do and whether you will be any good at it. Learning about AS and how it impacts on you as an individual is a big part of this and hugely important for many people. It is key to being able to ask for support and recognise your own limits before a crisis situation occurs. It may be necessary to find some support with this, as it can be hard to assess yourself in isolation. Speaking to other people about how you feel and how you cope can be useful. It can also be helpful to know that many people experience worry, anxiety and uncertainty about life and work and that you are not alone. They may just be better at hiding it.

Motivations for working

I had a suspicion before compiling this book that money wouldn't feature strongly as a reason for going to work for many people with AS, but it seems that I was wrong, as this was mentioned by a number of people as being an important motivator – although I suspect that the wording of the questionnaire was such that it did not elicit exactly what I was trying to get at. Many people mentioned that they worked for money, but this is money for survival, not money for impressing other people with a shiny car and big house. I still believe that the acquisition of money as a means of measuring social status and success could be less important to someone with AS than to someone without. Money used to buy possessions which demonstrate membership of a social group or set requires a sense of the existence of such groups and a sense of seeing yourself in comparison to others as a member (or not) of such a group. I believe that many with AS don't see themselves reflected in these societal norms and, although perhaps wishing to share friendships and relationships with other people, don't necessarily share the goals and aspirations of social status (or even understand or recognise their validity or existence). In the responses below, one person mentions working for social status (but gaining this from the job, not the money) and one mentions needing money to finance hobbies. There was no mention of needing money for a luxury lifestyle. The main motivators (besides earning money) were based on the enjoyment and non-financial gain provided by the job itself – providing it is the right job for the individual.

Key factors in motivation for working

- money – most commonly mentioned, but for practical survival rather than status or social advancement
- enjoyment of the work
- intellectual challenge
- prevention of boredom
- to be useful / gain sense of achievement.

Money is probably the reason that most people give for going to work – you only have to ask yourself: 'Would I do this for free?' to uncover your own motivations. Those with AS need to enjoy what they are doing to gather the motivation that makes the stress of work worthwhile, so the fact that several people said that they would work if they didn't have to, and that they worked for intellectual enjoyment as well as, or rather than, financial gain, is no surprise.

> Money for sustenance, money to finance hobbies. The challenge of learning how something works. The challenge to get so good at the job that I graduate on to bigger and better things. It is important in order to find things that make sense and the rationale of being able to work on the prevention of restlessness of sitting at home not doing anything. After two or three weeks if not doing anything, that sitting around gets tiring. (male, 30s)

> Social status is an important part of my motivation. I would feel ashamed just cashing in unemployment benefits without giving something back. I like learning new skills, but not too often. I need the comfort of old routines in between acquiring new skills. (male, 30s)

> I go to work to be normal. To be independent. (female, 20s)

> I think I have a lot of talent but I think it'll get strangled if I have to do something for the sake of it rather than for the task itself. (female, 20s)

Money. I have to live. I feel like I have a lot that would be useful. Skills others don't have, like being very analytic and very creative. Intellectually I have no problems, so I feel I need to make use of it. I would be unhappy if I couldn't do something productive. (female, 20s)

Money to spend on my hobbies and interests. I spend a lot of money each month on DVDs and books, which are horribly expensive. Of course, to prevent boredom and depression is extremely important for me. (male, 30s)

The praise I get for my work is something that makes me want to go to work and do even better than what I got praised for already. To experience new things, situations and assignments, as well as learning new skills and improving the ones I have already. (male, 20s)

In this society, the purpose of a job is always to 'make us money and then we'll give you some'. It's not because it's a valuable thing to do. (female, 20s)

In order of priority:

i)   to financially support my family
ii) to please my wife
iii) to give a good example to my children
iv) to earn social status
v)   to financially support my family. (male, 40s)

To prevent boredom is certainly high on the list, otherwise I'd just stay in bed with a laptop and a bottle of wine (it sounds like a bad thing, eh?!). I need enough money to live on and build a slush fund for the future. Professional status with my clients. I love the work, I'm bloody good at it, which is satisfying. (male, 40s)

To occupy my mind to stop me dwelling on stuff. To give me interesting stuff to do. Social interaction. To get money to spend on gadgets. (male, 40s)

Subverting the established order: using paid work time to do work that isn't what I'm paid for. (male, 60s)

Meeting my life-partner's expectations and sharing burden of household income. Feeding my high IQ through engaging with people with good minds, in shared activities or conversations. (male, 60s)

Getting access to free resources: photocopiers, telephones, email, libraries, pleasant workspace, paper and computers, etc. (male, 60s)

Personal interest in the subject. I understand that if I want to eat and live and survive, that I can directly influence that by earning a wage and allowing it to happen – that's a responsibility I understand. (male, 30s)

As I have a government pension I could work part time and have the same income but at the moment I choose not to do so. I continue to work full time as I quite enjoy the work, it gives my life structure and there is a national shortage of planners, so I'm not keen to effectively give colleagues more work. (male, 50s)

The challenge of overcoming the adversity with awkward people and situations. (male, 50s)

I couldn't give a rat's ass about money. I just do it for the love of computers. (female, 20s)

Money. That's the only reason I go to work. I could get all the other stuff elsewhere. (male, 30s)

If you didn't have to go to work, would you? What else would you do?

Perhaps those with AS have a reputation for being diligent, hard-working and enjoying intellectual stimulation and challenge, but does that mean that they would continue to seek this from paid employment if the financial need were not there? Is the love of the work and need to be useful enough for those with AS, or would they give it all up and travel the world, as many other people would, given the chance? Several people said that they would continue to go to work and others felt that it would be important to do something else, like study or write. Is this a reflection of greater importance being placed upon learning, usefulness and 'doing', as opposed to spending time with family and friends? Perhaps if social links are fewer, then work becomes more important. The idea of travelling the world alone may not hold so much appeal as sharing the experience with a friend or partner. This desire to keep busy and useful applies to many people who prefer to continue to be active after retirement.

> Work is important. I would grow tired of not having some-place where I am valued and expected to be every day. I would travel, money allowing, if I did not have to work. (male, 30s)

> I would continue to teach if I were able to select both the clientele and the curriculum. Otherwise I might return to my own studies, hopefully to PhD level, while modifying and driving performance cars. (male, 30s)

> Work is an important part of my weekly routine. I'm not good at keeping myself busy if I don't have a scheduled routine to fall back on. For example, I actually prefer work days to holidays. At holidays I sometimes fall into a kind of apathy because I don't have a scheduled reason to get out of bed. (male, 30s)

> I would not continue to work. Not in the sense that I do now, anyway. I would do a PhD in philosophy and write about ASD (autistic spectrum disorders) and ADHD (attention deficit hyperactivity disorder). I can't imagine having a job that I liked, although I would have to be very, very careful about boredom and depression if I didn't work. (female, 20s)

> I'd still work, I'd just stop charging for it so I didn't have to do the paperwork! I actually like my work and enjoy it. If I

didn't work I'd never get to see anyone from one week to the next and that wouldn't be a good thing. (male, 40s)

I would probably go to places and do stuff like make jewellery for a while or some analysis. I would need something to motivate me to go there. I don't really want to work, I want to produce something. I want to have a task that gets completed and feel useful. (female, 20s)

I would not work full time for someone else if not necessary. I would try to write for a living, perhaps, and just appreciate the simple pleasures in being alive. Travel and learning about other countries would be a big interest as long as I had someone to share this with. (male, 40s)

I will always work, if I don't have any daily goals set before me, I would lose the drive to do anything. I would sit and do nothing but watch the TV. I would even forget to eat each day, until I would realise that I was starving in the evening. (male, 30s)

I wouldn't go to work. I'd sit on my computer 24/7. It's actually my favourite place, my world. I'd go out and look at the garden now and again to make sure it's tidy, but otherwise it would be on the computer. Right now the safest place for me is on the computer. (male, 20s)

I'm thankful to have retired in this past year, aged 60. I relax and daydream and get up and go to bed when I feel ready. I meet friends for coffee conversations. I read some, and connect with people, known and unknown, over the internet. (male, 60s)

Currently I couldn't stomach a full day's or week's work of any kind and I don't expect to in the future. I spend a good proportion of each day reflecting and recuperating, just relishing the emotional space. (male, 60s)

Work is my primary access to social interaction and without it I suspect I would be far more isolated. As I get older I find the thought of retiring one day as daunting/scary, to be honest. (male 40s)

I'd spend my time doing my own projects. I've already written a few open source programmes. (male, 30s)

I wouldn't work. I would try and do something with my life that felt like it had relevance to my day-to-day life – like growing my own foodstuffs. Travel. (male, 30s)

My work is my life. I would need to replace work with other consuming passions such as numerology, astrology and writing. (male, 50s)

I don't have to work, but feel I need to. I do have hobbies. I am still interested in scientific subjects and would find it difficult to fill my time at home with purely domestic/garden work. (male, 60s)

I would endeavour to find a job where I could choose how much work I did, how much spare time I had, and achieved a feeling of genuine satisfaction from the work done. If this was not possible I would elect not to work. (male, 50s)

The perfect job

Is there any such thing as the perfect job? Or is this an oxymoron? A suitable job is one which allows best use of specific skills and minimises the areas of weakness. Lone working, excellent factual memory, logical analysis and problem-solving are likely strengths for someone with AS. Jobs which have been suggested to be more suitable for those with AS include:

- postman – lone working, lack of pressure, involves exercise

- gardener – lone working, lack of pressure, physical work (can be relaxing)

- IT technician – lone working, technical precision required, problem solving

- software engineer – problem solving, working to precise specifications

- photographer – creative, lone working, using technical skills

- researcher – analytical, focused, detail-driven

- accountant – proficiency with numbers, accuracy

- librarian – system focused, excellent factual memory

- piano tuner – perfect pitch, lack of pressure, lone working, specialist interest

- bookseller – specialist knowledge and interest, excellent factual memory.

Considering what factors your perfect job would comprise is an excellent way to work backwards from the required outcome (the ideal job) to look for work that would suit you and that might be available. Start with working out what you want and find something that fits, or almost fits, rather than seeing what there is and making the best of it. It's good to have in mind what you would like to do; it gives a greater sense of control, rather than having to put up with whatever you can find. This may be the reality right now, but it doesn't stop you making plans towards a more equitable situation in the future.

Make a list of all the 'essential' and 'desirable' criteria for your desired job. Start with what you love doing the most; your interests and hobbies. This may not be something that can earn you money, but there may be aspects of this that could form part of your daily work. Creative imagination is required to see the bigger picture and all possibilities. Enlist help for this if this feels difficult. The following questions may help you to define this job as much as you can. (This is looked at again in Chapter 5: Logistics – Finding a Job.) There are likely to be many other considerations to take into account:

- What do you enjoy doing most?

- How many hours would you be able to work?

- How far away from home could you travel?

- Do you want to work outdoors or indoors?

- Do you want to work in an office environment or in production?

- What physical/sensory factors would you need to consider (noise, lighting, etc.)?

- How much do you need to earn? Work out how much it costs you to live.

- What type of tasks would you want to be doing?

- Are you happy meeting new people, speaking at meetings and using the telephone?

- What qualifications would you need to obtain to be able to do this job? If you don't have the qualifications, how could you persuade a company that you can do the job?

- Would you be willing to study in your spare time to gain qualifications?

- Would you prefer to work alone or as part of a team?

- Would you want to be responsible for staff?

- What support would you need – writing a CV, telephoning the company for an application form, attending an interview, on-the-job support?

Respondents were asked to describe their perfect job, if they had the option to design such a thing. Naturally some found this difficult to do, given that it is an abstract concept and therefore not typically an AS strength, but most attempted it nevertheless. Some described their ideal job at great length, showing great imagination for an abstract concept. Factors such as control, limited contact with people and flexible working hours were mentioned by more than one respondent. Working part time may be a serious option for some with AS who find the draining demands of the workplace too exhausting for a full working week. This provides a clue that either full-time work or unemployment should not be seen as the only (all-or-nothing) alternatives available. For some, there seemed to be a sense of regret that they had not had the opportunity to fulfil their career dreams, and this was acknowledged as being due to a lack of support in earlier life. The interesting factor here, as in the answers to other questions, was the extent of self-awareness shown – people know exactly what they need. For those supporting people with AS into employment, it is important to ask your clients what they need, for they, above anyone else, will know their capabilities and limitations.

Key factors in defining the 'perfect job'

- flexible working conditions – hours and location
- autonomy
- enough money to alleviate financial concern
- control of schedule
- limited contact with other people.

> Something that I would be in control of how much external contact I would have with people. I would not have to get up at insane hours nor work insane numbers of hours. The work environment would be flexible. The pay would be such that I would not have to think about where my next meal is coming from. That is the part that I worry about. (male, 30s)

> I would serve in a small bookshop: perhaps part-owned by me, with someone else who had some business acumen dealing with that side of things. Perhaps a specialist bookshop in a small town. Just enough money so that it wouldn't be a source of anxiety for me. (male, 40s)

> How long is a piece of string? What colour should it be? Natural or man-made fibre? Sorry, facetious response to an impossible question. (male, 40s)

> If I were younger and had received help and encouragement during my education, I would aim to become a vet. My other ideal would have been to be a professional musician. (male, 60s)

> My ideal job would be writing software in my home and selling it. (male, 30s)

My dream job would be to support myself as a writer. If I tried to work from home I would likely get too little done, so I would need a private work office. I would need quietude to work but also company nearby if I felt like talking. I would need someone to check up on me maybe once a week to see how my work was going. It's important for me not to look bad in other people's eyes, so I would feel ashamed if I had nothing to show. It's easier for me to disappoint myself than to disappoint others. (male, 30s)

Flexitime. Programme or system admin work or technical support. With other people but not interacting continuously and not interfering idiotic management. (male, 30s)

I have no desire to design a perfect job – there is no such thing. (male, 50s)

My perfect job would most likely be as a part of a design/text team for either a computer game company or role-playing games company. I love working closely together with people that share the same passions as I do, where we're able to throw ideas, concepts and crazy thoughts around all day… I need a workplace where I feel at ease, where I can also do something else when my mind wanders too far away from the work I'm doing, like go play a video game or something like that…have a little fun. I'd prefer not to have my desk in an open space with lots of other desks, people walking around me all the time. But I'd definitely not want an office all by myself either. I'd like a space where I can put personal stuff, hang a picture up on the wall, decorate in my own style. Oh, and the job should have lots of perks, like free stuff. I love free stuff, especially if its stuff that's not released in stores yet and I get to play with it first. I'm like a little kid again when situations like that happen. Pay, as much as possible of course… Hours, well I work 20 hours now and that's an okay amount for me at the moment. However, if it's my dream job then I'd probably work a lot more than that. When something interests me, I give it everything I got and I'd probably not be able to quit after just five hours a day. (male, 20s)

I'm not sure Aspergers are very good at daydreaming, but my ideal job would make better use of my expertise in the legal aspects of planning. I'd want to be part of a team, colleagues it would be easy to get on with. Hours would be up to about 30 a week. (male, 50s)

Swanning around the world with my girl informing all the people of how wonderful life can be when you have the ear/mind/body of a beautiful woman to share/explore life's experiences. (male, 30s)

I would have wanted a job where I could set my own pace, and not be held back by slower colleagues. I would want a clear objective and access to any information or equipment I needed and I would want my manager to be willing to receive progress reports when I had reached an identifiable stage. I would want pleasant surroundings but to be able to shut my door when I needed to concentrate, but to open it when I wanted to be involved with others. I would like flexible hours, to be able to start early and finish early if I chose – for example, if I had an outside appointment that I wanted to attend, rather than have to take a day of leave. As to salary, I would like at least as much as my knowledge, training and qualifications should command, plus a financial recognition of my success at doing the job. (male, 70s)

Flexible working, whereby I can work in isolation when I need to (at home or in a quiet office) but also be around other people when I feel I am becoming isolated or need social contact. A role where people know clearly what my position is and where they know to come to me so that I do not have to market myself internally. (male, 40s)

Good daylight, plenty of 'breathing space', physical arrangement (furniture, etc.) open to individual choices… Quiet sitting areas nearby with comfy chairs and good coffee. Some green things. Sky. Flexible part- or full-time hours, including working at home. High degree of autonomy in identifying projects, designing the work structure and executing tasks. Liberal attitude to evaluating 'success' through dialogues rather than metrics… Enough time to become obsessive (e.g. with presentation details) and still get the job done! (male, 60s)

Actually I think it's good as I have it… I like the flexible time. I can choose when I work which fits in with me preferring to work late into the evening and night rather than the morning. When I work I'm well paid, but then working for an employer means you don't have to worry about getting clients. Ideally, I'd like to work two or three days for an employer or long-term contract and have the other two days to do [my own IT business]. (male, 40s)

Kitten stroker with philosophising. (female, 20s)

Most of the interaction with others would be via conference calls, as this suits my style. I would do consulting and travel to different areas to provide this service. The job is more important than the level of remuneration. If I feel valued then I remain loyal. (male, 40s)

My current job is perfect. I drive to the houses that I am scheduled to go to each day. I spend maybe two hours at a house. Any conversation is typically a question-and-answer about the product we are providing. I take my tools back to the shop and hand over my work for the next step to take place. The shop is union so hours and pay are taken care of. (male, 30s)

Forestry, horticulture, replenishment assistant (dogsbody) – I love all those jobs, but at the end of the day the whole idea of work for me is job satisfaction. To be able to be on my own, prioritise my own workload. I would be self-employed. I would spend 70 per cent of my life doing

hobbies, sport and outdoor pursuits and 30 per cent work.
(male, 20s)

Specialisterne ('The Specialists') – a specialist ASD employer

One company has turned upside down the whole idea of someone with
AS having to 'fit' into standard employment by designing a system that
fits around the needs of the individual and allows them to make best use
of their autistic characteristics by providing a supportive and stress-free
working environment.

> The plant *taraxacum officinale* [dandelion] is known to the
> majority as a very annoying weed – however, for the
> minority with special knowledge the very same plant is
> regarded as one of the most valuable herbs. But what is a
> weed – it is just a plant in an unwanted place. If you move the
> plant to a friendly environment it will give you access to its
> virtues and will become a most appreciated plant.

> The parallel between the dandelion case and Specialisterne
> is obvious. We create 'friendly' environments for our candi-
> dates and consultants with autism. By appreciating the par-
> ticular personalities we get access to the very special skills of
> people with autism. – Thorkil Sonne (company literature,
> 2008)

Background

Specialisterne (Danish for 'The Specialists'), based in Copenhagen,
Denmark, is a unique company, which utilises the specific skills of those
with ASD (autistic spectrum disorder), while not penalising them for
their weaker areas of functioning. The company was founded by Thorkil
Sonne after the diagnosis of his son with 'infantile autism with normal
intelligence' at the age of three. Thorkil became involved in autism
groups locally and met a number of young people and adults with ASD,
who were finding it difficult to get work that addressed their skills and
abilities. With a history of working in telecommunications, Thorkil

realised that there was a shortage of job opportunities for those with AS where individuals could use these strengths and also be supported in other areas. He also realised that IT was the industry that would meet these needs. Thorkil set up Specialisterne in 2004 to try and address this problem. The company now employs more than 40 consultants, all of whom have a diagnosis of ASD (usually Asperger Syndrome).

Specialisterne operates competitively in the IT sector and has a number of high-profile clients, including CSC (Computer Sciences Corporation – a global IT company which is Specialisterne's largest international client), Microsoft (who used the company to test Windows XP Media Centre), TDC (communications), Nordea (the largest bank in Scandinavia) and other major Danish IT companies. Services provided include software testing, data entry, fault detection and programming. The company prides itself on the quality of its services, which rely specifically on ASD characteristics of systemising, accuracy, repetition, memory and attention to detail.

> So far I haven't felt I had much of a choice in my career, this being the only autism-friendly company in the world. But I don't mind, I think we do important work here. Not just for our customers but for the autism community as well. (male, 30s)

> I have been unemployed for three years prior to working for Specialisterne. I spent my time at home, reading, writing, surfing the internet, playing computer games, and meeting once or twice a week with my friends to play 'Dungeons and Dragons'. I choose work because it gives me something to do every day, some structure and purpose. (male, 20s)

Why ASD and IT?

Specialisterne allows employees with ASD to do what they enjoy and are good at. These tasks are often ones that other people may find tedious and for which they may be less focused than required. These tasks exist in all business sectors, not just IT, and could provide enjoyable and fulfilling work for those with ASD.

> When I test software, I am basically expected to try and find
> all the defects possible in the programme. This means I am to
> try and break down the programme in any way I
> can…what's not to like about that? I also like that practically
> everything I'm asked to do, I do it better than expected and
> better than most anybody else would be able to do. (male,
> 20s)

Services which work with (rather than against) the skills of someone with
an ASD include:

- Software fault detection – those with ASD may have the
  visual focus, attention to details and ability to locate errors
  that others with more 'bigger picture' focus could miss.
  They are also able to remember what they have seen and
  identify discrepancies.

- Programming – those with ASD work in a logical and
  systematic way, which makes for efficient and effective
  programming.

- Software testing requiring repetition – some with ASD
  enjoy repetitive tasks and find them relaxing and
  enjoyable.

- Data entry – what is sometimes referred to as 'fascination'
  can keep some with ASD focused for longer periods than
  someone without ASD, who may become quickly
  distracted and bored.

- Accuracy – high attention to detail and desire for precision
  and perfection allows those with ASD to maintain high
  levels of accuracy in their work when inputting data and
  programming. Clients have reported 10 times higher
  accuracy than with non-ASD workers.

The expertise of their unique workforce has enabled the company to
compete for major contracts on an equal basis in the marketplace, based
on quality and competence, rather than charity. The social responsibility
aspect for the client is an added benefit of employing Specialisterne.

> The company always asks my opinion before giving me a new work assignment. If I don't like a particular kind of work they usually find someone else to do it. I test programmes and manuals and describe what flaws I find. (male, 30s)

> I am employed as an IT consultant. I test software for our clients, both at our office and also as an external consultant with the client. I am also one of Specialisterne's primary translators regarding translations in English. (male, 30s)

One client reported that other workers lose concentration on repetitive tasks, but described the way that ASD employees from Specialisterne worked as 'breathtaking' and their work 'as close to perfect as you can get'. They also commented on their fantastic abilities to remember every screen image (Computer Sciences Corporation company literature, 2007).

Working for Specialisterne

> Specialisterne care for their employees first and the clients second. (Specialisterne employee)

Employees work 20–30 hours per week, usually five hours per day, as it is recognised that they may not have the capacity to be fully effective working full-time hours. They are supported through extensive planning of their workload and given the clear and detailed instructions that they need.

> Our assignments are usually described very well and detailed and always written down for us. (male, 20s)

The main difficulties identified are the different 'culture' that the person with ASD is working within, which requires this structure in order to minimise their stress and maximise their potential. As Thorkil says, 'It's very hard to get a real chance to demonstrate your virtues if you always are in working environments where you are not understood, or worse: always misunderstood. The traditional, mainstream labour market requires flexible, empathic employees who master stress situations.'

> Specialisterne is all about giving support for us. They make sure that if we are going out to a new client as external consultants, then the client will be informed of the special circumstances that apply to each individual employee. (male, 20s)

At Specialisterne ASD is the 'norm', with the working environment established to meet their needs. Those with ASD are the majority, and the role of the non-ASD staff members is to provide the required support.

> Work allows me to have a purpose each day, and they understand if I need a day off, or if something is troubling me and I need some space for dealing with such matters. (male, 20s)

The ASD employees do not have to worry about how to interact socially, as they are not expected to excel in this area. Workplace communication is kept clear and straightforward, and bluntness and directness are expected. In fact, some managers say that they find it refreshing that opinions are clearly stated with no hidden agendas. Individuals are free to take breaks and lunch with colleagues or alone, as they prefer, but many make friendships with colleagues which provide social activities outside of work.

> I'm not expected to be sociable when I don't want to. If I just concentrate on my work and ignore my co-workers, no one gets offended. (male, 30s)

> The fact that every employee here has an AS diagnosis makes social relationships a lot easier. Our interests are 99 per cent of the time extremely similar, and if we don't want to have any social relationship that day, then nobody is forced to talk to anyone. (male, 20s)

A large amount of the work takes place in the client's workplace, and so environmental issues need to be taken into account in discussion with the client. Employees often prefer to work listening to music through headphones to shut out external noise.

> It is simply the best job I have ever had. The company focuses a lot on all the various quirks we employees have.

> Such as specific requirements for our workspace, environment, how many hours we work each day, and so on and so forth. (male, 20s)

Recruitment and selection

Individuals applying to work at Specialisterne need to have a diagnosis of ASD and the ability to access state disability employment benefits, which will contribute to the costs of their employment. They join a labour market preparation programme by completing an application form. Those with few or no qualifications are not excluded from applying, as the company recognises that those with ASD have often not had the opportunity to work, owing to the social nature of most jobs. Candidates are assessed on their motivation, vocational skills and work ability using a range of tools, in a way that does not rely on interview skills, which can disadvantage those with ASD. The use of Lego Mindstorms, a robotic programming system, is one means of assessment used to measure a range of skills, including what motivates the individual, their learning profile, how they react when a task is too difficult or too easy, their ability to problem solve and follow instructions. Lego is the perfect medium to test the required skills without the need for verbal expression and social skills.

> I had a job interview with Specialisterne, though I don't remember much of it. It went pretty straightforward, a formality really. They, of course, were aware of me having AS and as such it was okay for me to be honest about which things would work for me and which things would not work for me. It felt like they really wanted me for who I am, not just what I can do, and so they got the whole package. (male, 20s)

This allows candidates to receive the appropriate training and be placed in the job that best supports their abilities. Candidates then work alongside experienced employees to experience the work environment, while being supported by managers as they progress through the labour market preparation programme, which can take five months to complete. After this time, the person may begin work at Specialisterne, begin a college course to gain a qualification in IT, or be placed with another company.

The future

The company has ambitious plans for the future. Thorkil believes that people with ASD and the needs of business are the same the world over; it is only cultural and welfare systems and provision that differ. This can be addressed by adapting the basic Specialisterne model to each specific country. The company hopes to take the Specialisterne model to other countries and employ over 1000 people with AS in this way. His vision is to prove that those with autism can take an equal part in society and that they can bring new skills to the business market. The benefit to those with ASD is an increase in self-esteem, as they have a positive experience of being understood and realise that they are able to perform valuable tasks to a very high standard, which is respected by the business community. The company was visited by European Commissioner Vladimir Spidla, who said:

> Specialisterne shows that there is a place for everybody in the labour market. Integration of people with disabilities into the first labour market can be a clear win–win situation for employees and employer if all potentials are fully used.

Thorkil sums this up: 'Lessons [we have] learned are that under the right circumstances people with ASD can perform valuable tasks as good as – and often better than – people without ASD.'

The final word, however, goes to a Specialisterne employee:

> It is not the people having Asperger Syndrome that prevents themselves from moving forward in life, it is the world around them that does. People fail to understand that having Asperger's is not a disease, it's a gift. People who have AS should be showered with gifts (especially new toys not released in stores yet) and given priority in those specific jobs where they do what they do best, instead of being ostracised by mainstream mentalities who haven't got a clue what immense resources people with AS could provide from them. (male, 20s)

4

Early Experiences and Personal Circumstances

Childhood experiences

AS is a lifelong condition and, therefore, those affected by it will have spent many years dealing with its effects before they become a potential employee/worker as an adult. The adult with AS contemplating work has previously been a child and adolescent with AS – often unwittingly – and these experiences have shaped them in a number of ways both good and bad, and these will affect their adult perceptions. Our early experiences help us to build a worldview of whether we live in a positive and support-ive world, or a bewildering and rejecting one. Many of those with AS are likely to have decided upon the latter. Few of those questioned had received any support for their AS. This was not even a possibility for many, as they remained undiagnosed until adulthood. Most were educated in standard mainstream school, and this is the case with most children diagnosed with AS today. For the majority of children with AS, mainstream education should be achievable with appropriate support and training of staff. Intellectually, those with AS are usually able to manage the level of work required. In fact, it is often quoted that people with AS have 'above-average intelligence', which must be galling to those who don't fit this profile but are expected to perform miraculous feats with numbers (as seen in a very small percentage of people with autism, known as 'savants'). I think that many with AS are very knowledgeable within their chosen fields and areas of interests, but this may be more of a data storage skill rather than a creative and imaginative one. They tend to adopt a more rational and logical viewpoint, which can make information easier to classify and decode, but this may be balanced by different abilities in creative thought. This will vary from one person to another. The diagnostic criteria for AS lead us to believe that those with a learning disability (often signified as an IQ score of less than 70) do not qualify as having AS. They would be classified as having classic autism, and so the lower IQ range is eliminated from the picture. I believe that those with AS have abilities and intelligences that run across a wide range and that one score, such as IQ, is not an adequate measure of the entire capabilities of a person. Having high abilities in academia may not be useful if a person is unable to access the learning environment owing to sensory sensitivities, or lacking in social or practical living skills or 'common sense'. A general lack of support and understanding of the true nature of their different behaviour is the main message from those consulted.

Bullying

Bullying is so commonly experienced within the AS population that it is rare to meet someone who hasn't suffered this fate either at school or elsewhere – including the workplace. It is estimated that up to 90 per cent of those with AS experience bullying (Attwood 2006), but my own experience would put this figure even higher. Sadly, children (and adults) are very adept at spotting someone who is less able to 'fit' socially and a person with AS can become an easy target for those with more advanced social techniques available to them, such as deception, sarcasm and non-verbal skills. The person with AS can appear innocent and naïve and will believe what is told to them, which makes them vulnerable. These experiences of being bullied can continue throughout a person's life, into adulthood and at work and in social situations. Workplace bullying was mentioned by several of the people questioned, and I have met others who have clearly been bullied but have not recognised the malicious intent of their colleagues. They were sometimes grateful to have some form of social attention and described the behaviour as something like 'general banter' rather than the bullying that it was. Even if they had been aware that it wasn't appropriate, they would have been unlikely to have the communication and social skills to deal with it effectively. Skills for 're-pairing' social situations are an area of difficulty for many with AS. The effects of childhood bullying and exploitation can have huge effects on a person and influence all of their relationships, as they have learned from an early age that they are not deserving of respect and friendship. Many of those questioned reported horror stories about schooling and also about being bullied out of their jobs by managers in adulthood. The experiences of children with AS today will impact on the self-esteem of the adults with AS of tomorrow.

> I got into a fight at the beginning of each year of school, where someone gave me too much grief. After going berserk during these fights, people had enough sense to leave me alone. Example: I was thrown off the balcony level of the cafeteria, ran back up the steps, charged headlong into my enemy, throwing him off the balcony, then jumped down after him, pummelling him senseless until the gym coach pulled me off. (male, 30s)

> I was bullied through primary school. I was very thin and small, so I was easy pickings. When I was 15 or 16, however, I finally managed to stand up for myself and caused one of the bullies to be kicked out of school. After that time I have always been able to respond in kind to those who try to bully me or any of my friends. I am very good with words and good at finding the words that hurt the particular person the most, so it's rare that I find someone who can better me in arguments and discussions. (male, 20s)

> I wasn't a very popular boy but I didn't feel bullied either. I didn't feel all that different from other children my age until puberty. Back then I wasn't really aware of how I was different, but I could feel that I was. I didn't (and still don't) have much intuitive social understanding. I have to learn social issues as intellectual concepts in order to incorporate them. (male, 30s)

> Bullying was a problem. I was a nerd through high school, and for the most part I did not fare well with the social angles. My closest friend through that time was someone I

am beginning to wonder whether he is on the [autistic] spectrum as well. (male, 30s)

Was bullied briefly but learnt to fight back – too well! Serial monogamist with friends. Frequent meltdowns among crowds and under peer pressure. (male, 40s)

I was isolated. I didn't know how to relate to people. I tried without success. I was bullied, so occasionally I would get into fights with some kids because they had initially started to antagonise me, but the teachers almost always came down on the kids' side. As a result, I was further isolated. (male, 40s)

I was the odd one out. I didn't realise I was a person until 14. I just liked the lessons. I had been bullied the whole time but I didn't care. I didn't want them to like me and didn't care that they didn't. It wasn't until I became a teenager that I started to care. (female, 20s)

I was bullied quite a lot throughout my schooling. Mostly verbally. One day some of my schoolmates showed me a dead rabbit, but I don't know why. (male, 40s)

Bullying – boys and girls, due to height, talking to self, highly intelligent. Called me stupid, annoying, dumb, idiot, prat – even though I was doing their homework. Hyperactive; hard to focus mind. The few friends I had were the bullies. (male, 20s)

Bloody terrible time and this is hard to write about. Obviously you've come across this before, otherwise the questions wouldn't be here. I didn't really have any friends at all, maybe a couple – then again I'd say the same today. Yeah, bullying was bad and I still don't understand: why pick on me? Break time I used to hide where I didn't think I'd be found and read a book. That's OK for a few days, but every day for ten years or whatever it gets a bit wearisome. (male, 40s)

I didn't play with other children and spent breaks 'helping the teacher'. I had no friends outside school or inside. Fortunately I wasn't picked on or bullied. I was just a brainbox, and quiet ('shy'). (male, 60s)

I cannot recall any bullying incidents. I recall my father saying, 'You won't be able to use your brain so you will need to use your hands.' (male, 60s)

I wasn't bullied per se, I was excluded and laughed at more than anything. (female, 20s)

I was bullied at every school I went to. In each instance, I hurt the bully so badly that nobody messed with me again. In each instance, I'd get into trouble, and the teachers wouldn't accept my obvious explanation that the only way to stop a bully is to beat the shit out of him. (male, 30s)

I sang in a world-renowned choir and wrote prizewinning articles entered in school competitions. I avoided much bullying, as being in the choir enabled me to stay out of the playground for much of the time (rehearsing and just sitting in the music department). (male, 40s)

Bullying most certainly, whether that is as a result of AS or the obvious uncomfortableness, or whether the uncomfortableness is as a result of the AS, all of this is unknown. (male, 30s)

People kept slagging me off for being weird. (female, 20s)

In order to make use of these experiences, it is necessary to acknowledge their existence and the extent of their occurrence. As an employer, it is important to be vigilant in identifying how less socially adept employees are treated and how they cope. It is important to handle these situations sensitively, and failure to do so can make the situation worse for the individual. Awareness of AS and why the person seems somewhat naïve amid workplace interaction can help colleagues to see that there is a reason for this lack of understanding and not that the person is 'stupid', which is how they may perceive them. For this reason, I would advocate disclosure whenever possible, as this provides a name and a framework for explaining why you behave as you do. Ignorance, sadly, causes people to draw their own conclusions, which are usually mistaken.

Behaviour at school

It is interesting to note how easily, in some cases, those with AS navigated school, or at least appeared to do so. Perhaps the style of teaching was more structured and involved more rote learning in the past, which would suit a person with AS better. This was certainly my experience of school, growing up in the 1970s and 1980s. The physical environment of the classroom at that time is likely to have been less stimulating to the senses; there would have been no computers, bright colours and expectations of moving seats and teamworking. This could have implications as to why some children now growing up with AS struggle to cope with school and become either withdrawn or disruptive – and why children nowadays are identified and diagnosed earlier (as a consequence of this inability to cope), whereas similarly affected children may have gone unnoticed in the past.

This may, in turn, have a consequence for employment. A more successful education is likely to have fostered a greater ability to endure and tolerate the workplace. If young people struggle to manage school and some fail to achieve qualifications which reflect their abilities, as well as failing to learn the workplace skills taught at school – following instructions, punctuality, politeness and co-operation – they will be further hindered at work. The older people consulted certainly had difficulties at school, but seemed to overcome these in order to continue on to employment without diagnosis or support. Diagnosis and knowledge of all types of disability and diversity have increased over time and so, where people might have been labelled as 'naughty' and punished in the past, they are now more likely to have their behaviour looked into and the true cause identified. This doesn't always happen, but at least there is more awareness.

Those questioned were asked if their behaviour at school was noticed as being different in any way, bearing in mind that many had had no diagnosis at this stage of their lives. They were also asked whether they had received any support at school. Universally, they had not.

At college I had a problem relating to anyone at all. General feeling that others were beneath me in regards to computers and the course as a whole. Similar problem at university. (male, 30s)

When I first went to school I had literally no experience of spending time with other children, away from adults of my family, and I cried heartbroken every morning when my mother left me at the school entrance. (male, 60s)

Being a 'loner', sometimes perceived to be a smartass. (male, 40s)

I was always regarded as a nerd and a bit of an outsider. My teachers complained about seeing potential in me, but I didn't follow up on it. I was often labelled as being lazy, and at the time, I believed it to be true. Nothing was ever done about it; neither my parents nor my teachers did anything to help in any way. (male, 20s)

I refused to be taught by those I did not respect. Educational psychologist saw me every two years, gave me an IQ test and then lectured me on 'having the IQ of an Oxbridge student and wasting my talents'. (male, 40s)

I was noted as being a very nervous child, and I would often miss school through feeling sick through anxiety. No assistance asked for or received – I just got on with it. (male, 40s)

My crying at the start of the day took up a lot of my secondary headteacher's time, to his frustration and annoyance. But after that quietened I was never seen as any kind of problem – I was the school's star pupil. (male, 60s)

I mostly kept to myself, but I was able to figure out the correct behaviour when playing with other children, although I couldn't make stuff up like they could. I liked Lego, not cops and robbers. (male, 30s)

Always struggled to make friends, so would stick to only a couple of friends that I made early on, usually also high achievers like me. (male, 40s)

Personal circumstances

When people were asked about their current living arrangements and their level of satisfaction with these, there was a range of responses. Typically, those who were married, retired, and who had previously experienced successful working lives were the most content. Those who reported difficulties with managing domestic organisation and practical life skills sometimes had high-level jobs for international organisations, which goes to show that the skills and abilities required to perform well in one arena are not the same as those for another. It should also not be assumed that a person who can manage a multimillion-pound contract can organise their own laundry.

Just over 50 per cent of those questioned were, or had been, married, the remainder living alone, with parents or in shared accommodation. Out of the 12 people in their twenties and thirties, ten of those were not in relationships or married (83%). Of those aged 40 or above, 9 out of 13 people (69%) were, or had been, married and had the support of a wife or partner. I suspect that this sample group is not typical of the AS population, many of whom are believed to not be in relationships or married. Having a supportive partner or parent may help to ease some of the load of 'life', share domestic responsibilities and allow the person to focus their energies on work. In terms of how satisfied people were with their living circumstances, money was mentioned most often as a barrier to change in living circumstances, but most people expressed some satisfaction with their current situation. Relationship difficulties, needing solitude and privacy, wanting to move out of the family home and being independent were also important issues mentioned.

5

Logistics – Finding a Job

Choosing what job to do

When given a large number of career options, none of which you have any experience of, it can be very difficult, and often overwhelming, to know where to begin. How can a person know what job they want to do when they have never tried any job at all? This has been the response of some people with AS that I spoke to. One man, when asked what type of work he would like to look for, said, 'I don't know. Can't you just tell me what to do?' The current trend for support is to provide person-centred, non-directive support which allows choice and efficacy for the individual. Choice can be very difficult for someone with AS, who struggles with abstract and imaginative thought. Imagining the realities and consequences of working in a supermarket or making metal screws on a production line may feel impossible and so passivity may ensue. Because one cannot imagine anything different than what one has now there may be no impetus or ability to change. This was apparent in the responses where a sense of drift, accident and trial and error determined career, rather than any one job being a determined goal. Actually doing the work is perhaps the only way to find out if it is something that is tolerable or enjoyable for any length of time, with this limited imagination. Those questioned were asked whether they had chosen their careers and how they had made this choice. Interest in a specific topic played a part for some people and an awareness of some of their own needs, such as not being near people, was also apparent, even though some people did not know that they had AS at the time they made the decision.

Yes [I chose] the big picture of order and detail. No [I didn't choose] specifically. I know I like the patterns that exist in accounting, however, I knew that I was not going to be handling insane amounts of overtime in a near toxic political environment. Office politics is a worrisome issue. (male, 30s)

Accident mainly. I had a couple of offers from the arms industry so I went there, playing with very expensive equipment which never got used much. I stayed doing pretty much the same thing until I realised I was good at computer systems and also systems engineering in business. I kind of fell into it by accident when I got involved in a business re-engineering exercise and put the systems in to support all the new processes. (male, 40s)

I do what I do because I don't know what else to do. It was felt (by my mum) that this was something I could cope with, and haven't known how to change it, despite going to university to study a non-related subject. I have very few skills and I just about get by. (male, 20s)

I have always worked in bookshops as I have a love of books and find it easy to sell them. I could never feel the same about shoes, for example. I can use love of books as a base, and then learn specific subjects about which the books may be written (modern art, languages, theatre, genealogy). (male, 40s)

I was asked to teach one module initially as emergency cover and found that I enjoyed it and was good at it. (male, 40s)

I like working on my own. I do like physical work. I like work which challenges me, but it has to be on my terms. I don't like too many rules and regulations which slow the job down. (male, 20s)

Personal interest in the subject, autonomy, possibility of travel (for, although my life is tailored towards stress reduction, I am very aware that nothing begets nothing, and so when it suits me to, I will allow a rise in stress levels in order to progress, this relates to the travel aspect of my working life: it's relatively safe and at someone else's expense). (male, 30s)

I have drifted on the tide of life, guided only by the vagaries of chance and circumstance, accepting my position, whatever it may be, with equanimity. (male, 30s)

Tried working in stores first, didn't work. Tried corporate work, didn't work. Tried residential/light commercial work, loved it. Got jobs where I was driving from site to site and having minimal interaction with home owners, I will never take any other kind of job. My current job is a personal interest for me. I would probably do the work for nothing if I didn't need the money. (male, 30s)

Minimum effort, maximum gain. (male, 40s)

I didn't [choose], I used nepotism to get sponsorship with the company my dad worked at, and have accidentally slipped from role to role, slowly evolving my career with no real plan at all… However, I have always tried to pick and choose jobs that I felt were very stimulating, that I was excited about. (male, 40s)

I never really took any notice of anybody else's notions of employment – it was always 'me and MY work'. And 'my' work was very often at a tangent to my employer's idea of what the work was. Bridging this gap has always been difficult and a strain. Ultimately – after 40 years of working life – I gave up on it. (male, 60s)

I chose to do planning at college as it was a good general subject, and subsequently specialised in dealing with planning applications. Post diagnosis I have realised that my particular interest in planning law is an Asperger interest. (male, 50s)

Personal interest and not having to deal with the public. (male, 40s)

In Chapter 3, under the topic of 'The perfect job', it is suggested that you make a list of the requirements for your ideal job (see page 76), and this may be of some help when thinking about what type of work to do. Obviously, what jobs you can select are limited by what is available within your given geographical parameters, experience and qualifications.

The job that you choose now doesn't have to be the job you do forever. You can change jobs, careers or direction at any time. Not having the skills for your perfect job doesn't mean that you cannot work towards it over time, and having a goal for the future can be helpful in keeping you motivated to work towards it in small steps. Pinning something on the wall to remind you of where you would like to be will help. Read articles in newspapers or magazines about different jobs, cut them out and keep them. This assembles more data to get a better idea of what different jobs might entail.

Being realistic is important. It is unlikely that you will become an astronaut, for example, without many years of study, training and work. It is also not for those who are affected by claustrophobia, don't like to be away from home or have restricted eating and toilet habits! Every job has consequences. It may provide a big pay cheque, but may come with circumstances that you would find intolerable.

Look in newspapers and on the internet to see what jobs are available and what other people do. Often companies have profiles of some employees and you can see what they do and what their work history was that got them there. Research is useful in thinking how you would like to spend your days.

If it is really impossible to decide what job to try, perhaps voluntary work could be an option. There are often many organisations looking for volunteers in a wide range of roles: IT skills, gardening, publishing a newsletter, accounts, art and music projects, etc. If you do not have a volunteer agency near you, look in the telephone directory or internet for local charities, or ask family members if they know anyone who needs some help. The only way to increase confidence, experience and skills is to do something. The longer a person is unemployed, the harder it is for them to return to work. Doing something is usually better than doing nothing, as it gives you a reason to get up in the morning, prevents isolation and gives a sense of achievement.

Key points for choosing jobs

- Research what types of jobs exist – ask other people about their jobs.

- Think about the consequences of doing certain jobs – good and bad.

- Search for available jobs and try to think if you could do them.

- Request work experience in a company that interests you to see what it would be like to work there.

- Look around you at the jobs that people do and see what their work involves, and think whether you could do their job.

- Ask people that you know what job they think you would be good at.

- List all of your skills and interests – the job for you may become obvious from this list.

- Ask others to help you to list your skills – it can be hard to know what you are good at.

- Try a number of volunteer jobs to get a better idea of what types of activities and environments you enjoy and work well in.

- Any activity or research that you do today will be a step towards finding work that suits you.

- Complete free online psychometric tests, quizzes and profiles relating to career types to give you some suggestions. Do not take these too literally or seriously as they are just a guide.

- Get careers advice from a professional. There may be free support available from your Careers Service or Jobcentre.

Applying for jobs

Once some effort has been made to narrow down the choice of work, it is time to consider actually applying for a job. Little AS-specific support in searching and applying for work had been available to help those responding to my questions. This may partly be related to the ages of the sample, as few of them had known about their AS when first looking for work. There seems to have been a strong sense of rationale and logic involved in selecting jobs, with people clearly assessing whether their skills and experience matched that of the job. This is probably no different to anyone else in this matter, although perhaps the risk-taking 'just go for it' and 'blag it' element is less apparent.

> I have never felt confident in applying for any job and have usually been pushed/cajoled by others. (male, 40s)

> It has been extremely difficult for me to apply for jobs. I don't have many concrete qualifications or experience and I am very bad at selling myself in applying for jobs. (male, 20s)

> I feel it is very limited how much information I get from reading a job ad, and I'm very bad at making contact with a place I'm interested in for further information. I have received no support in searching for jobs ever and I think it might have been a big help for me to have support in finding a job. (male, 30s)

> I wasn't sure what jobs to apply for because I didn't understand the reasons for my problems, and so wasn't sure what kinds of jobs I was fit for or not. (male, 30s)

> I know what I am good at and I kind of know what I need. I just don't know what job I would fit in to. (female, 20s)

> I compare the skill set listed with my own, compile a list of possibilities and then go down the list, starting with the closest match. (male, 30s)

I may have been picky, but not noticeable. Ones [jobs] which I think I will enjoy and which will use my skills. The Employment Office is known as the Joke Factory. (male, 40s)

Looking for new jobs and applying for them has always been an ordeal. With little sense of norms and expectations, no strategic–pragmatic sense of career, and no ambition except to resist being forced to be not-myself, for much of my life I've entertained absurd fantasies of what kind of labour somebody might actually pay me to do. (male, 60s)

Selecting jobs is very hard. I was thrown out of the Jobcentre during an interview with an employment officer because I had no idea how to narrow down the field of potential jobs in response to her 'what are you prepared to do?' question. To me, I don't know what I want to do, but I am prepared to do virtually anything. I have no idea what jobs there are and what they mean; I only know what I do. I couldn't work out how to narrow down the possible field of options so she asked me if I wanted to be there, and I replied that I didn't. This was the truth; it was sunny outside and I didn't want to be there. I am told that the correct answer would have been that I did want to be there, but that would have been a lie. (female, 20s)

The only criterion I've ever used in choosing jobs to apply for is: can I expect to get away with it? Is there a chance they'll give me the job? Can I look plausible? Job search support would have been completely pointless. An acting coach might have been better. (male, 60s)

When applying [for jobs] I got wonderful support from [disability employment scheme] who suggested I apply to my current employer. Still very unsure as to what I am suited for, having drunk alcohol to enable me to work in the past. (male, 40s)

Can I drive around and have minimal interaction with people? (male, 30s)

My brain kind of does a 50/50. It knows that some jobs I am qualified for and I should go for it. Then I think 'There might be more people than I expected' so I shouldn't go for it. Other times I think 'I could do with a change, I should go for it and blag it'. Then I think 'What if I can't blag it?' and I think I should stay where I am. (male, 20s)

I tend to apply for a job where I can offer previous experience in the relevant area, rather than trying for something I may be capable of but can offer no proof of previous ability. (male, 30s)

How close is the job defined and how close to what I have done before? That is the key definition for me. If it is completely alien or asks for experiences I don't have, then I will pass on the job. (male, 30s)

I have always had difficulty in working out what jobs would work for me. When young, I took random risks based upon a few simple criteria and often found the positions wrong, so had to move again. Often been reactive, responding to headhunters or opportunities that came my way through people I knew. Most recently I have been very focused on the exact role I want and indeed maybe too much so. I once had job search assistance when made redundant. It was helpful. At the time I did not know I was Aspergers. Maybe now I know who I am, I can do better... (male, 40s)

[I am] only limited by the nature of the job, if the subject matter doesn't grab then I wouldn't apply – but isn't that the same for everyone? A long time ago I received a job offer in the financial markets in London, but couldn't accept for the subject matter didn't inspire me. That overrode the option of earning more money. (male, 30s)

The application process itself will differ from job to job, but one important fact to remember is to do as you are asked. If you are asked not to send a CV (*curriculum vitae*, a report of your personal details, education and employment history), don't send a CV. If you are asked to use black pen, use black pen. Make sure that your application is received before the deadline. Ridiculous as it sounds, the inability to follow instructions like these may lead to your being dismissed from the pile of applications received from people who did do as they were asked. The ability to follow instructions and submit the application on time are skills which an employer will want to see evidence of, and this is your first opportunity to demonstrate these.

Writing a CV

It is worth trying to find some support in compiling a CV or completing an application form. There are free CV templates on the internet which can give an idea of how to structure a CV. You can also find other people's CVs online on their personal websites, which will help to determine what type of information to include. Basically, it is a document to show all that is good about you and to convince an employer that they would like to know more about you at an interview. It is your first and main opportunity to sell yourself. Do not be afraid to sound immodest or 'blow your own trumpet' – that is what everyone else will have done, so you need to do it as well. This doesn't mean that you should lie in your CV – but you should make the truth look as good as it can. Find someone to help you with this, as it is often a tough concept for someone with AS to grasp. There are many guides to CV writing, which offer different strategies and tips. Keeping it fairly short is usually a good idea: one to two pages should be enough. An employer won't have time to read reams of information when they may have many applications to sift through. And make sure it gets there on time, or it will probably go straight into the bin.

What to include on a CV

Advice varies on what to include on your CV, but it should certainly contain all of the following:

- name, address and contact details (phone, email)
- date of birth

- education history – schools, colleges and qualifications gained

- employment history – jobs, voluntary work, work experience placements, in chronological order, including brief description of major achievements and tasks in each of these roles

- other qualifications and roles – from personal interests (e.g. sailing instructor)

- personal interests – this is to show what useful skills you may have from your hobbies and leisure activities.

With your CV, you may be asked to submit a covering letter. This is a letter introducing yourself to the company. Always make sure you address it personally to the correct person. In this letter, which will usually only be one A4 side long, you should explain that you wish to apply for the job advertised and that you have enclosed your CV. You should also briefly outline why you wish to be considered for the position and what skills you have to do it. The covering letter is very important as it will be read before your CV, and so should be neat, well laid out and well presented.

Key points for CVs/job applications

- Provide the information exactly in the format that you are asked to.

- This is your opportunity to tell the employer how well suited you are to the job.

- Keep it short.

- Make sure it is there before the deadline.

Interviews

Interviews are a classic area of difficulty for a person with AS. There are many issues involved which could cause confusion and anxiety:

- organisation and planning – arriving on time

- managing public transport and finding location

- understanding the appropriate dress code

- environmental issues – room temperature, lighting, noise

- nonverbal language – eye contact, body language, picking up cues

- limited ability to 'lie' or exaggerate skills in order to give best impression

- understanding requirements of questions – which may be broad, abstract or hypothetical

- asking appropriate questions; not asking inappropriate questions

- feigning interest in the interviewer, making small talk

- short-term memory issues, e.g. forgetting interviewer's name.

As an employer, if an applicant has disclosed their AS to you, you need to be aware of these issues and address them. Contacting the person before the interview and asking them what support they might need would be helpful. Provide detailed written information about what the interview process will involve and how long it will take, and indications of the type of questions that will be asked. An interview should not be a test of interview skills, but a test of the skills required to do the job. A practical trial or test may be a better way of assessing this in someone who doesn't perform well with verbal expression. This is a reasonable adjustment which does not discriminate on the grounds of a person's disability.

The following are comments regarding interviews from those questioned, some of whom felt that they performed well at interview. Whether they were successful in getting the job, or whether this view was shared by the interviewer, is not known.

> My technical abilities have always done the speaking for me. One interviewer said: 'we will work on your personality later, but we need your skills now.' (male, 30s)

> I feel I've always done well enough in interviews and don't think any lack of job offer has been solely down to perfor-

mance in interview situation, but probably down to lack of relevant experience. (male, 30s)

I think my weaknesses are that I'm not good at looking people in the eye during interviews and I can come off as unemotional (uninterested) because I don't show my feelings in a way that is easily discernible for people who don't know me. (male, 30s)

I get extremely nervous going to an interview. I've learned to calm down more over the years, but I still get uncomfortable. I find it difficult to understand what it is they're really looking for during a job interview. I try mostly to be myself with everything that's me, my strengths, my flaws. I'm very honest when people ask me something, which I have a feeling isn't the best quality for a job interview. (male, 20s)

I am good at interviews. (male, 50s)

I have never gained work by interview. Each job I have had has been gained by personal recommendation. In those job interviews I have attended, I have felt awkward and clumsy. I am either too timid or too aggressive to have impressed the panel. This was always an enigma to me until I learned of the traits associated with AS and recognised them in myself. (male, 40s)

I blagged it. It's pure luck. I absolutely hate interviews. AS and interviews are not a good mix. I have researched interview techniques. We are all doomed. Anyone with autism is very lucky to get the job, I have decided. I am surprised I have managed to get the jobs I have had. I have been myself in interviews. Too honest, too open; said very odd things. It's hard to figure out what they want to hear and what I want to say. (male, 20s)

I haven't had many issues in conventional interviews. But I have real difficulty in 'competence based' interviews. This is where interviewers demand instances of situations in which you have done 'x' and exactly what you have done to achieve 'x'. I find that my memory simply does not keep records in this way. I do things by hunch and intuition and every situation is a new one. I don't keep templates and modify them...and I have no ability to set 'goals' that I then fix on in order to achieve them. In my life I just take one step after another, navigating from point to point in an emergent landscape. My only resource is a sense of 'this doesn't feel good yet so I won't stay here, I'll move over there and see if that gets any better'. I understand this to be my own core form of the 'weak central coherence' of AS. (male, 60s)

I have usually had tranquilisers in my system when interviewed in the past. Always found them hugely stressful and wished I had never applied when having them. When given advice before interviewed, I know I would never have used the 'tricks' advised to me, off my own bat. They would simply never have occurred to me. (male, 40s)

In a recent job interview situation, I was required to give instances of situations in which I'd been successful in many things that I have been successful in – e.g. working in teams, providing services. I could not come up with examples of anything. Fortunately I had a chance to rehearse (it was an agency placement, and the agency rehearsed me for the interview). I spent an entire day drawing a historical chart of all the different kinds of things that I'd 'delivered' in all my jobs across 35 years, and classifying them by the kinds of 'competence' headings that the interviewer was likely to use. I took the list into the interview room with me. It did the job. (male, 60s)

The job interview is the worst, because you're expected to put on this song and dance to garner their favour. I have to be VERY VERY VERY careful not to correct the interviewer's mistakes or misconceptions, because doing that always guarantees that they won't like me, and I won't get the job. It's always got to be 'Yes, sir, yes sir, three bags full, sir', i.e. lying. And lying grates on me like nails on a chalkboard. It's also hard to do those little things that make the interviewer like you. I understand that it's those little things that can make or break an interview, but I can never manage to do them correctly, or figure out when the timing is right. (male, 30s)

I've had an extremely high rate of obtaining interviews, but a low rate of getting jobs, and I put this down to AS problems. (male 50s)

I have problems when questions aren't well defined and are really broad. Don't know how to narrow it down. I have ten thoughts at once and don't know which one is appropriate. I tend to say 'I don't know'. (male, 20s)

Some positive, some negative. Open-ended questions with no 'pitch and catch' and leaving me looking for words is an impossible situation. I find too often that the interviewer asks questions that may be close-ended to them, but I would find open-ended and therefore have no correct or biased answer that works in the interviewer's favour. AS does create issues in terms of dealing with the interviewer. The interviewer with an incompatible voice or question style that leaves me looking for answers to questions that are not rehearsed is another matter altogether. (male, 30s)

Ill at ease. Not a natural conversationalist. Most jobs I got from having contacts. (male, 40s)

Sometimes my interviews have been informal and then have gone well. With formal interviews I often come over as arrogant and have been ruled out of jobs based upon assumptions that I would not be a good fit. I always used to feel I was self-selecting myself out but now I realise it was more than that. (male, 40s)

It seems that having personal contacts who can introduce you to an employer is useful, but not everyone has access to these. Making people aware that you are looking for work may help, as other people won't necessarily know this unless you tell them. This may also help you avoid a formal interview if you are known to someone who knows the employer.

In an ideal world, requesting a work trial or some other way of demonstrating your abilities to do the job would be the best way forward, but this is not always possible. There are many resources on interview skills, but caution should be exercised about trying too hard to be someone or something that you will not be able to sustain if you get the job. If you find eye contact painful or pointless, it will be obvious to the interviewer that you are not doing it naturally and you may look more odd than by just not looking at all. Even if you don't wish to disclose your AS, you can mention to the interviewer that you find eye contact difficult, so please could they excuse you not looking at them very much. People are very accepting once they know what it is that they are dealing with. By taking these kinds of preventative measures, you are stopping the interviewer from making their natural assumptions about you – which are likely to be that you are rude, deceitful or arrogant for not looking at them.

Asking for questions to be given to you in advance, finding out what the procedure for the interview appointment will be, and getting as much information about the company as possible, will all help to get a good grasp of what will happen. If you do decide to disclose your AS prior to the interview, it would be advisable to provide the company with some information about AS, as they may have no idea what it is and how it affects a person. The National Autistic Society produces information sheets and a 'Looking for Staff?' leaflet which explains the benefits of employing a person with AS.

Interview tips

- Be on time (or early) – this is very important. Lateness is likely to be seen as a sign of lack of interest in the job, or lack of motivation.

- Practise the route and journey beforehand to ensure you have left yourself enough time.

- Shower, shave, wash and brush hair, put on clean, smart clothes, smart shoes – look your best, as these things often matter to those interviewing you.

- Learn about the company and the job so you can ask questions and show that you have done your research – this shows that you are keen and interested.

- If you don't understand a question, ask politely for it to be rephrased.

- Try to retain concentration on what the interviewer is saying.

- Usually more than a one-word answer is required as the interviewer will want you to give an example or details relating to the questions.

- Usually an answer which involves you talking for five minutes or more is too long.

- Stay focused on the question and do not go off track and talk about other things.

- Do not say anything negative about the job or the company, even if you think it.

- If asked about your plans for the future, do not say that you only plan to work there for a few months, even if this is the case, as this is likely to lose you the job.

- Prepare some things to say which make you sound enthusiastic about working for the company.

- Remember – an interview is a test of how well the interviewer thinks you can do the job and how well you will fit in with the company, and you only have a limited amount of time to demonstrate this – use it well.

Motivation to look for work

It is sometimes reported that those with AS suffer from inertia and get 'stuck' in familiar patterns and behaviours which they find almost impossible to move away from. This may be partly as a result of avoiding risk and change, and also of difficulty in comprehending the consequences of action (or non-action). A person may not be able to work out or predict the possible outcomes of not working, which may include eviction for non-payment of housing costs, debt, ill-health (depression, malnutrition), having no TV or computer as the electricity bill might not get paid, isolation, lack of intellectual or physical stimulation. There may be a desire to change a situation but the person cannot see any of the possible options for change, like buying a newspaper to look for a job, joining a college course to learn new skills, or contacting someone who could help with some advice. Most people I questioned had some level of difficulty with making the initial shift from stasis into movement, although, once started, they found it easier to continue. It is not change itself that causes the problem, it is transition – the process of moving from one circumstance to another. Once the new situation is reached, it is no longer 'new' and is therefore familiar.

It makes me physically ill to even think about it. (male, 30s)

I find job-seeking extremely difficult. I am aware that I have very poor telephone skills and avoid using it as much as possible. Joblessness is probably the hardest rut to get out of. (male, 40s)

I often need other people to give me the push to move forward. Left on my own I tend to stick to my comfortable routines. (male, 30s)

I find it extremely difficult to motivate myself to apply for jobs, and I don't like talking on the telephone generally. As for moving my life forward, previously it has often been because of outside influences, like the local authority, who have been blocking my path forward. I have a lot of issues with the local authorities because of all the trouble I've been put through by their bureaucracy and general insanity. They have probably put more fuel on my depression than any other single person or situation has ever done. But yes, I do feel it is hard to make my life move forward on my own as well. (male, 20s)

Motivation within the job is easy. I can look at a set of goals and think 'I can do that'. Motivating myself to get a job is very hard. I can find problems and fix them, but I can't do that to myself. (male, 30s)

The difficulty is in the motivation to do it, not the actual doing, once motivated. (male, 50s)

I have problems getting round to doing stuff. Everything seems to be tangling me. Having to split my attention between lots of different things. Once I start something, it is often OK. I have problems motivating myself on my own. I tend to get more done if someone is guiding me, keeping me on task. (female, 20s)

There's always a 'hump' to get over, before initiating live contact... In writing applications for jobs, the 'hump' is: Oh my god, who do I have to pretend to be this time? Is the real me ever going to get recognised? Who the fuck are the grey, amorphous ones I'm trying to please this time? (male, 60s)

I HATE applying for jobs. Or anything else for that matter. I avoid the phone whenever I can. Email is better. With email I have time to consider what I'm going to say, and read and reread and reread again to make sure there's nothing offensive in there. I still fret about it afterwards, though, and go back to check what I wrote, just in case there's something that could be taken the wrong way. (male, 30s)

Very easy [to motivate myself]. The work ethic is ingrained. (male, 70s)

I often find myself stuck in a problem with no idea how to move forward. I seem to have difficulties with lots of things, and these often (to my mind) block any exit routes. That said, perseverance has done me well and I hope will continue to do so in the future. (female, 20s)

I find this very hard to motivate myself for. I usually do it to satisfy others who make demands, or because I wanted to be seen to be trying, and to fit in. (male, 40s)

'Moving my life forward' is a phrase that makes no sense to me [this was the phrase used in the questionnaire]. I have no sense that progress is possible. Life – in the sense of external achievement – is simply a matter of struggling and more struggling, with whatever gets thrown up carelessly by the world. Progress lies within, in becoming able to respond with equanimity to these endless, thoughtless and inconsiderate challenges. (male, 60s)

It has been hard to work out what I want to do, it's hard to apply proactively and easier to be reactive. Plus I hate phoning people I don't know. I often feel I am stalling my entire life, not moving anything forwards because it seems too much, or at the other extreme rushing headlong without thinking through. (male, 40s)

Making telephone calls is the hard part, swallowing me up and hoping that the person on the other end of the phone is not too overwhelming or overbearing. That part is the most frustrating part of the exchange for me. (male, 30s)

There is no easy way to get motivated apart from just doing it – something, anything. Doing nothing usually means that nothing will change. The only way for things to change is to do something to change them. I have been looked at in puzzlement when I have discussed these concepts with some people with AS, who can have the belief that 'life just happens' and that they must passively accept this. Accepting that you can change your situation means taking responsibility for the position you are in now and choosing (yes, choosing) to do something about it. Focus on the end result: the money, the end to boredom, the new PC, or whatever it is that makes you want to get out and get a job.

Disclosure

Jane Meyerding (2006) cites around a third of the people she spoke to as having 'come out' at work. She reports that this is more likely to be an informal process, one-to-one with colleagues, rather than a management-led approach. There is undoubtedly an element of fear of the consequences in revealing one's true nature. Unfortunately, for many people with AS, whether disclosure is active or not, the individuals may struggle to conceal their differences in a workplace that causes them stress and confusion. Not disclosing can mean that colleagues make assumptions about the reasons for certain behaviour ('weirdness' or 'stupidity', for example) and react accordingly, which does not make the job any easier. Even if you do not disclose your disability at the time of recruitment, you can do so at any point during your time at work, and your employer must accommodate your needs. It is never too late to ask for adjustments to be made and you do not have to continue to struggle. My question asked those with AS if they had ever disclosed their condition at any place of work and/or whether they would consider doing so in the future. The majority of the answers given demonstrate either a mistrust of how an employer would react to disclosure, or a strong belief that they can manage unaided. This implies that some of those responding had found a low stress environment in which they could survive and potentially thrive.

> Only diagnosed three years ago and feared that it would be held against me in getting an interview. (male, 40s)

> My wife expected me to do that when I got the diagnosis. I would not disclose AS unless it affected my job performance. (male, 50s)

> I disclosed to my employer upon diagnosis as I thought it might help my students. (I was doing a deal of work in additional learning support.) The surprising result (to me) was that I have not been asked to do *any* similar work since. (male, 40s)

> I wasn't aware of AS until my last work setting, which was very shortlived. Yes, in future I would disclose AS. Previously I have disclosed a history of mental disability (in the form of depression and anxiety)…and I hope that pitching this in terms of AS might be a little easier. But maybe not? AS is hard for people to understand – and instances are very diverse, which is confusing. (male, 60s)

> I have told them, but haven't asked for help. I told them on advice from [a] psychologist. I'm not sure whether I'd disclose again. I do not explain, verbally, very well and am

often stymied by my lack of verbal coherency and clarity. If I thought I could adequately explain, and that I would not be judged or ridiculed as a result, then I probably would. But, I think I am describing another world from this one. (female, 20s)

I have told the office manager at one of my major clients because I needed an ally and felt I could trust her. I was having difficulties with people complaining I hadn't done stuff, when I hadn't been asked to. For example:

> 'It would be nice if I had a data card so I could work on the train coming into the office.'

> 'Yes, it would.'

Then after two weeks I got a complaint that I hadn't ordered it and set it up. Well, duh! If you'd asked me to do it, I would have.

It went well actually, and she looks out for me and translates when required, and if someone's joking lets me know. (male, 40s)

I am fortunate to have a very understanding boss who takes the view he works for his staff, so I have disclosed to him and discussed with some work colleagues that I trust. I have not officially notified the company and have no plans to do so, as in the current environment I feel it would cause more problems than it would solve. (male, 40s)

[Disclosure] not appropriate, I was self-diagnosed after retirement. I am not sure whether I would have disclosed it, had I known. (male, 70s)

[Disclosed] to some. Some with whom I have long established working relationships are not open-minded enough to appreciate that my 'strangeness' or 'unconventionalness' might have a name and a root cause. Although this serves to undermine the significance that AS plays in my life, I have to accept that for these people it's obviously not so significant to them that I have a name for me. Interestingly, the only people I've been able to share the information with are the two females I work with. (male, 30s)

The management don't want me to tell my colleagues that I have AS. They say that I have to have an official diagnosis before I tell anyone at work. I think the whole world needs to know about AS and autism in general. (male, 20s)

I consider it essential so they understand me and problems that occur can be allowed for and dealt with better. (male, 50s)

It's not their business. I would only discuss this if it became a problem concerning the employer. (male, 50s)

Once you divulge something like that, everyone starts to fixate on the differences. It strains relationships that are already hard enough to maintain. I made the mistake of telling some of my friends last year when I found out I had AS, and now I regret doing that. (male, 30s)

I don't want people to know at work, because it changes things, usually for the worse. (male, 40s)

It makes me unsafe to admit to it unless things are stable and sound. I fear that there would be retaliations and I would get to be the first to go when jobs get cut and people are let go; they let the 'challenged' one go first, not asking questions, just firing. (male, 30s)

I have told them (managers) and I genuinely think they don't believe me. (male, 20s)

I would disclose in future and be quite open about it because it makes my life easier – I can be myself. I would have to. To me it's an obligation to myself – they would have to accept me. (male, 20s)

By disclosing AS to an employer (or potential employer), you ensure that adequate support is provided as a preventative measure – before the stress or other problems arise. Also, there is the wider issue that if no one discloses, then awareness of the positive skills and abilities of people with AS does not increase, which does not help those in the future seeking work. This is a contentious point since it places the onus on individuals with AS now to pave the way for future generations, but without increasing disclosure, I'm not sure how things will change. Employers will continue not to understand the condition or the benefits of employing someone with AS, and the situation will not improve. Only around 22 per cent of those asked had told their employer about their AS. There seems to be a reactive rather than a proactive approach, i.e. they would disclose if they needed to. Unfortunately, as in the case study of Simon (in Chapter 2, see pp.51–60), that may be too late. I wonder if here there is an element of inability to see consequences until they have happened, such that some people cannot see that preventing potential problems through awareness and adjustments may be preferable to waiting for the worst to happen. Still, it must be said that many of the individuals employing this tactic have managed successful careers – but at what personal cost in terms of stress?

Employers – what if you suspect an employee has AS?

If an employee has not disclosed and yet you suspect that they have AS and it is causing them problems at work that you cannot ignore, what do you do?

This is a very difficult and sensitive situation, which needs to be handled with care. I have had a number of employers contact me regarding a staff member who they believe has AS, asking me what they should do. First, it is important to remember that AS is officially a medical condition and can only be clinically diagnosed by a qualified physician, so the suspicions of an employer must be aired very carefully. Second, before saying or doing anything, try to put yourself in the employee's place and imagine how you would feel if you boss told you that he/she thought you had autism and that was the first you knew about it. The likelihood is that you would be shocked, upset, angry and defensive. The approach you use depends on whether you feel that the person is aware that they have difficulties and what kind of working relationship you have with them.

- Can you deal with the job-related issues without mentioning your suspicions of AS?

- What is your motivation for telling someone you believe they may have AS?

- Will it help this person to know? If so, in what ways?

- What will happen if the person rejects your suggestions or is very offended?

If a colleague or workmate is determined that the subject needs to be tackled with the employee and they want to air their thoughts, it is suggested that the employer has an informal, private and relaxed conversation in which he/she casually mentions the possibility that the person may be exhibiting some aspects of AS and gives the complainer some information on AS characteristics to take away and read at their leisure. Alternatively, the employer could ask the employee concerned if he/she would be willing to have a chat to an AS specialist who might be able to give a more informed opinion.

It is important for the person concerned to know how the employer feels that this potential AS relates to their job and what issues have arisen that need addressing. If the person does have AS, they will not be able to process this huge piece of new information immediately, and will be unlikely to agree with it. They may not appreciate what has been said, but may be intrigued enough to consider the information they have been given at a later date. It is important to reassure the person that their employment will not be jeopardised by this discovery and that there are no negative implications to having AS. Arrangements should be made for a follow-up meeting to discuss the person's thoughts on the subject in two to three weeks' time. The subject should not be discussed or brought up in the meantime.

If the person dismisses the idea of AS at the follow-up meeting, the subject should be dropped. Only where there is a health and safety issue, or other serious implication, should further action be taken. This is a very delicate matter and extreme caution must be exercised to adhere to appropriate legal and ethical guidelines and procedures when approaching an employee.

If the employee agrees that they may have AS, the employer must then provide support in accessing a diagnosis (if one is required), training staff, providing mentoring or other specialist support, and ensuring that the workplace meets the needs of the individual.

6

Guidance and Training – Specialist Support for Individuals and Services

It is reported that few people with AS find successful employment without specialist support (Powell 2002) and that more with AS would be able to retain work if they were better supported.

General support available

Of those questioned, few were receiving any type of specialist support – for employment or otherwise. Most had found their own way, generally due to their age – AS was not known about when they were starting out in their working lives. Around 28 per cent of the group questioned were aged 50 or above. Their experience of work and society may have been quite different from that of young people today. Choices were perhaps fewer and jobs more stable, with many being 'jobs for life', which is far less likely these days.

Many did not want support in their workplace, sometimes for fear of being discriminated against. Some said they had tried to disclose to colleagues and had negative reactions. These are the responses of a small group of people, many of whom had managed to find work with no support and no diagnosis. (Legally, employers are required to support those who disclose a disability or health condition, and it is advisable to do so in the majority of circumstances.) In terms of the support people did receive, for many it seems that their parents, spouses or partners had been the main source of help and support, which can be quite a big responsibility. For those who do not have partners, it is all the more important to seek outside help, as managing alone can be too much to cope with.

Some people did have access to specialist services. (This was especially true of the two Danish respondents who both had a support worker.)

> Mental health therapist, wife/partner, mother, in dealing with the times that are difficult for me to work with. My frustration is not being able to share when something is not working. I have a hard time when I am not able to share that something is giving me the chills or discomfort in any way, shape or form. (male, 30s)

> My wife has been my support and she helps me with anything I find difficult. (male, 60s)

> My mother sometimes helps me with chores like cleaning and she tries to make me get out more. I'm a member of an autism association and a contact meets me once a week to talk and help me with paperwork. (male, 30s)

> I have a support worker who visits me once a week. He helps me with almost anything I need help for. Helps me make sure any bills are paid in time, talks to the local authorities if I need them to do something for me. He helps me organise my life in general, so I have the structure I need in order to be able to cope with all the normalities of life. My family live quite far away from me, but they support me in any way they can. Often we just talk on the phone, but once in a while they come to visit me. If I need to refill my freezer with foodstuff they supply me with generally high quality meat, spice and whatever else I might need. (male, 20s)

> My parents live nearby. I don't really have much support because I don't ever ask for help. (male, 30s)

> I have lots of friends who have AS. I have student support at uni[versity] and a mentor who helps me to do stuff I find

confusing, like talking to people and filling in forms. (female, 20s)

I have had lots of support. My mom has always been there to mop up the mess and the tears that have resulted from my misunderstanding the world. I have one friend who tolerates, and sometimes accepts, my differences and we get on very well. A psychiatrist and psychologist provide professional support. They have been fantastic. They have taught me that it is OK to be me, and that different is not necessarily worse or abnormal. (female, 20s)

I see a learning disability charity worker twice a week to help me with practical tasks. I attend a social support group once a week. (male, 50s)

Couple of people speak to me on the phone. Have ASpire [AS charity] mentor. Friends on phone try to help me understand what is going on. Mentor helps me to 'organise stuff in my head'. (female, 20s)

Family works with me occasionally, making sure I get a checklist with priorities set. Friends help ease me into social setting and know not to push too much. (male, 30s)

I do get support from the people with whom I live, often in practical matters, such as fixing things which are broken or organising my life. My family are a great source of emotional and financial support. I have a partner who is learning very quickly about the help that I find useful and is willing and able to supply it when she can. (male, 40s)

My dad is trying but wants me to be me, but not talk to myself. No one understands it, except [AS support worker]. Helps to clear my mind, every time I leave I am focused. Helps to talk to someone who understands AS in a way no one else does. Makes me feel normal again. Online AS forums. (male, 20s)

None [support]. My wife just keeps finding things wrong. (male, 50s)

Wife discovered AS and she helps change behavioural patterns. There is much improvement in communication skills and social situations. (male, 60s)

During my working life I had the committed and loving support of my very capable, non-AS wife... My wife basically took responsibility for dealing with the outside world and the future: buying a house, acquiring a car... I had three breakdowns during my married years and in each case my wife took up the slack when I've been unable to work... I depended entirely – unhealthily – on my wife for perspective, support, guidance, work-sharing, fun, relaxation, confession, companionship and continuity of human connections. (male, 60s)

Visited by Prospects [National Autistic Society employment service] every six months. Attend Autism Asperger Group monthly and other seminars, etc. as and when opportunity presents itself. Currently having short counselling course through GP (doctor). (male, 50s)

My sole support is my partner, who is very knowledgeable of the subject (AS). She is also extremely supportive, non-judgemental and accepting. With her understanding, this one person allows me to feel some connection with the world I've never experienced before. (male, 30s)

Since last year I have been meeting with a psychologist, my company insurance covers the cost of a formal assessment but not treatment, so this costs me a lot of money. I am lucky to have a small number of friends who have been very understanding and now they know [about AS diagnosis] are making a special effort to include me in activities. (male, 40s)

None. My wife looks after the finances mainly and she does her best to cope with the house, etc. (male, 40s)

Case study: ASpire – mentoring support for adults with Asperger Syndrome

ASpire is a voluntary sector project, based in Brighton and Hove, East Sussex, which provides mentoring support for adults with AS. While the project is not primarily focused on employment support, the skills learned by its users are essential in allowing them to progress towards work, if that is what they desire. ASpire's client group are adults with AS or similar social skills issues and the project works in two distinct ways:

1. Project users are supported by volunteer mentors who are recruited, trained and supervised by the project. These mentors work one-to-one with a project user over an extended period of time, providing support with a range of goals and needs initiated by the user. These may include job search, independent living skills, money management or social skills. The mentor is often the main social contact for the person with AS, and so performs a befriending function as well.

2. The project provides AS awareness training to organisations that may work with, or support, those with AS. Previous clients include universities, colleges, victim support and witness services, employment and careers services, employers, residential homes and a range of other service providers.

By providing this holistic approach and supporting both individuals with AS and external organisations who support them, ASpire attempts to provide an AS-friendly environment surrounding the individual, where everyone the person meets or works with has at least a basic awareness of AS. The support provided relies on the commitment of the volunteer mentors, who give their time unpaid to the project. Few of the service users reach employment quickly because they have so far to go to get there, as many have had no previous support. They may only recently have had a diagnosis, in adulthood, after many years of confusion, low confidence and low self-esteem. The project attempts to empower individuals by teaching skills and strategies to move towards independence, rather than engendering a 'helping', parental mentality. Service users are involved in all aspects of the project and also attend social activities and discussion groups if they wish. There is no time limit to their involvement with the project; they can continue to have a mentor for as long as they choose, which is an important factor often missing from support services. It takes a long time for some with AS to be ready to make the changes they want to make – a typical three- or six-month programme is not long enough to encourage and embed any new behaviour or raise confidence. Many people with AS would benefit from ongoing support, as there are always new situations which they may find hard to manage alone. The mentor also acts as an advocate in education, employment or official situations, supporting the person to gain access to the right services. The project is overrun with requests from new people with AS for support, but has only limited resources to do so.

This type of support seems to meet the needs of those with AS, as it provides practical guidance plus the opportunity to interact socially and practise skills with an accepting, aware person. For those in relationships who were questioned, it seemed that the spouse or partner played very much the same role for them.

An evaluation report of the project's work (MacDonald 2007), which involved interviewing project users, found that the greatest reported improvements were in 'confidence' (75%) and 'social interaction' (67%). Around 50 per cent of those asked reported improvements in more practical areas, such as employment, education and managing money. Many of those working with the project are supported slowly into gaining the skills required for work. Some may not achieve this all their lives.

Voluntary work

For some, voluntary work is a safe, first step into employment and mentors have supported their mentees into finding suitable organisations to work for. ASpire has strong links with the local volunteer centre and encourages volunteering as a path to work. This allows an element of choice so that people can select organisations and charities which have tasks that reflect their interests and allow them to try new activities without harming their CV or employment prospects. Voluntary placements allow someone to gain experience, often in a patient and understanding environment. When I went to visit one charity shop manager to explain about AS, as she was due to have a young man start work at her shop, she said something like: 'We don't care what he's got, we get all sorts here: heroin addicts, schizophrenics, alcoholics – they're all equally welcome'. Her attitude was one of acceptance of anyone, regardless of their background or difference. Two years on, the person with AS still works at the shop one day a week, despite having obtained a paid part-time job, and is known for his expertise in organising the stock, testing all the videos and making sure that the jigsaws have no pieces missing.

Often the role of the mentor is simply to be someone to discuss ideas and thoughts with; someone to provide another perspective on a situation. If you have no one to talk to, you only have your own input on anything. In a couple of cases, individuals who began with the project as users have progressed to become mentors themselves and support others with AS; they wanted to 'give something back' to people who may be finding life difficult, as they know how it feels to be isolated and low.

AS training for services and employers

As well as providing support for the individual, it is also recommended that organisations, support workers and family members should have access to AS awareness training to enable appropriate care and support. Powell (2002) suggests that all services and employers supporting those with AS should be adequately trained in awareness of AS and also in the job-related needs of these service users. He lists a comprehensive set of recommendations on the type of information and training that services could receive, which includes: 'selling' the skills of a person with AS to an employer, understanding the specific qualities and weaknesses of those with AS, and how to recognise when someone is ready for work. He also outlines a training strategy for those providing support services to people with AS. This clearly states that: 'The complexity of Asperger Syndrome requires that people who work alongside those with the condition are regularly and specifically trained to provide good quality care and support' (p.19). One service quoted by Powell (Avon Asperger Syndrome Project) reported that the most common request made by adults with AS using services was for support from someone who understood their condition.

Powell also identifies a number of training principles which are recommended. Some of these are summarised below.

- There is a need for expert input into the development of AS training.

- There is a recommendation for two tiers of training provision – AS awareness training and job-specific or specialist training.

- Trainers need to be experienced and preferably still working with those with AS or autism.

- Those with AS, or their family members, should contribute to training sessions.

Powell recommends that awareness training should cover the theory of the autistic spectrum and provide some basic practical strategies. The requirements of specialist job training will vary depending on the job role of the participants, and need to be tailored to meet these needs. This training may take up to three days.

As well as providing awareness training, it is important not to ignore other life skills. As stated in the introduction to this book – if someone cannot cope with life, they will be unable to work. Practical life skills need to be assessed to ensure that the basics of life are being adequately covered. Only 3 per cent of those with AS are said to be living independently (Barnard *et al.* 2001), which suggests that there are huge numbers of people who are unable to manage daily life. The types of skills which need to be assessed and, if necessary, taught may include:

- managing money – shopping, budgeting and banking

- hygiene – both personal and domestic; keeping self and home clean

- safety – home and personal safety, security and recognising dangerous situations

- public transport – coping with sensory overload, learning routes and reading timetables

- organisation – remembering appointments and schedules

- social skills – prevention of social isolation, managing friendships and relationships, understanding non-AS social rules.

These skills are not learned overnight and require long-term, consistent, AS-focused support. Without these skills, a person with AS will find it very difficult to even consider looking for a job, let alone have the confidence and ability to remain in a work and social environment for several hours each day.

Workplace support

Overwhelmingly, the vast majority of those questioned received no support whatsoever, probably because most had not disclosed any issues that required adjustment. Several people did not want help, but preferred to cope on their own. For those with AS, who often value what they are able to do rather than who they are as people, I wonder if accepting help (or admitting the need for it) would make them feel that they were less capable. There is a stubbornness that suggests that someone would rather walk out of a job and risk hardship and unemployment than admit to having a condition which can be disabling in certain circumstances:

> I tend to deal well with chaos in the workplace but not in my family life. (male, 50s)

> My feelings on this are mixed because on one hand I would like support. I would like a mentor who knew the difficulties that I have; someone I could go to for clarification – for example, when my job role changes inexplicably and implicitly... On the other hand, I also have a desire to be seen as normal. This desire has driven me through situations that I have been tempted to give up in. Perhaps it is just pride. Perhaps it is a fear of the stigma that is attached to mental disorders, especially disorders that are largely couched in popular myth; *Rain Man* [film about man with autism], severe autism, schizophrenia, etc. I do not wish to be misunderstood in this way, and so choose to expend more effort than people can possibly appreciate in getting by. (female, 20s)

> The greatest 'support' has always been autonomy to do things my own way without close supervision, and to an

extent, to do what I decided was worth doing. I always found schedules, procedures and specifications [of work content] to be burdens that are hard to tolerate. (male, 60s)

To have things written down. Precise instructions. Timetables, structure and predictable workload. (male, 20s)

I do not receive any support for AS in my job. Given that my hours are extremely fluid, it is difficult to ask for support (though I know it should be available) because such 'help' could easily include a lessening of my workload, which I can ill afford. If pressed, I feel a counsellor in whom I could confide my issues and concerns would be of the greatest benefit. (male, 40s)

I receive no support as I have not disclosed my AS, due to fear that I wouldn't be given the job. Now I feel it is too late to inform them, although others have insisted that this wouldn't be a problem, and I should do so. (male, 40s)

Tight technical specifications, stating exact requirements of piece of work. AS awareness training for colleagues and managers. Predictable workload. Schedules/timetables. (male, 30s)

Prospects [National Autistic Society employment service] supports and provides basic training for new colleagues when needed. Managers are generally aware of issues (and I will often draw attention to them) and are sympathetic. (male, 50s)

I prefer to cope on my own initiative. (male, 50s)

Variety could help maintain my interest. Can't deal with boredom. Written instructions. (female, 20s)

The best help for me is a solid schedule that doesn't get changed much. (male, 30s)

Knowing what my job looks like at the beginning of the job. Knowing what each week looks like at the beginning of the week. Written instructions of what is expected is valuable because it gives an 'I want this' angle to things. When the workload gets bizarre, knowing when to say 'this is getting bizarre or stupid' is a valuable thing for me. (male, 30s)

… my new boss is very understanding and I have told a few work friends so they can try to involve me in stuff, or at least understand when I withdraw. (male, 30s)

I have a colleague who has a father with AS and she now understands me. She goes round telling people to leave me alone and do what I need to do. (male, 20s)

I would like to be given a list of jobs rather than be told how long a job will take me – they tell me it will take 20 minutes – the job takes as long as it's going to take. This drives me mad. Being asked to do the jobs and being left alone to do them. (male, 20s)

Case study: National Autistic Society Prospects

We are encouraged by the increasing commitment and engagement of employers. (David Perkins, manager, NAS Prospects (London) team, personal communication, 2008).

Finding specialist employment support is very helpful to many with AS, but unfortunately this type of service is sparse. The work of such programmes can help to inform more generic employment service providers and ensure that the service they provide does not exclude those with AS from success.

The National Autistic Society (UK) runs a programme of employment support for adults with autism and AS. This is based in a number of cities across the UK, and serves individuals from these locations. It is the largest and most comprehensive service of this type in the UK and is organised in such a way as to provide person-centred, flexible support that meets the needs of the person (as opposed to the needs of the service, which can sometimes be the case!).

The London-based service works with around 320 clients each year, with support ranging from intermittent, in-work support up to intensive training programmes over a course of weeks. The service employs ten employment consultants and support workers, who each have a caseload of clients to support.

A vital aspect of the service is the longer-term nature of support available; clients can occasionally continue to be supported over a period in excess of two years, which may be necessary for someone with autism or AS whose skills and confidence need to be developed before they feel able to work. (Shorter programmes may abandon the individual after six months or so – perhaps just at the point when they were ready to really make progress.) The support is tailored to fit the client and is reduced as they become able to manage their work more independently, but remaining in the background in case of difficulties which arise. This may be as little as a telephone call every few months, but is important as a reassuring measure. It is worth mentioning that most clients do not require support over a two-year period, but find suitable work at an earlier stage.

For those not initially ready for paid employment, there are programmes available to build confidence and job skills and undertake long-term voluntary placements – sometimes with high-profile companies – to enhance future job prospects, gain valuable work experience and add to the person's CV. Alongside these specific, job-related programmes, individual support is also available to students with AS needing additional support around their AS while studying.

Individuals are often self-referred or otherwise referred by employment advisors and other agencies. The initial assessment process involves clear discussion of expectations of the service. Some people with AS may have unrealistic beliefs about their abilities or what the service can do for them. Setting clear boundaries and managing expectations is important in minimising disappointment and frustration.

The types of people who work with Prospects are mostly in their twenties and thirties, with an overall range from teens to fifties. (Some people are typically not diagnosed until adulthood, but this may change as early diagnosis becomes more prevalent.)

The success rate of the service is impressive: each year, around 40 per cent of clients obtain employment after being supported by the programme. The London service has exceeded its annual target, with over 50 people finding new jobs this year, and a further 75 receiving workplace support.

Clients with AS or autism are advised to disclose their difference as this allows a consultant to contact the employer to discuss required adjustments before they commence work. These requirements are often quite small, such as having written instructions, a designated desk in a quieter area, or flexible hours which mean that the person can avoid travelling during rush hour on crowded transport. These small measures can mean the difference between someone being able to work, or leaving their job owing to stress. The person with AS or autism may find it hard to discuss their needs and may go off sick with stress, or simply walk out of the job, never to return. Intervention from an employment consultant can prevent this situation from escalating, or even occurring in the first place.

The types of jobs that those with AS using Prospects tend to prefer often involve administration tasks, such as filing and data entry – activities which typically do not require a lot of interaction with the public. Tasks which are process driven and have a clear order and completion are also preferred. Some individuals, however, actively seek retail work to increase their interaction with people and improve social skills.

Some individuals experience difficulties after they've begun a job, and may ask their consultant to act as an intermediary between them and the employer to resolve these issues. For some people, their job is the only social contact that they have. They may live with their parents and have few same age peers, so their job may be a strong focus in their lives. This, combined with a difficulty in reading social messages, can mean that they misunderstand social relationships at work and may misjudge their approaches to colleagues.

Other issues often involve stress and anxiety, which many people would consider to be disproportionate to the situation. People with AS often become highly stressed by unpredictability and changes at work or the travel involved in getting there.

Prospects 'sells' the benefits of diversity to an employer by emphasising the skills and qualities of an employee with AS. Many employers experience difficulties with high staff turnover and large recruitment costs. It is known that if an employee with AS is happy with their work, they are less likely to leave than a non-autistic employee, as they prefer known situations and do not necessarily seek variety and change.

The experience of Prospects is that employers are much more aware of disability legislation than in the past: they know that they are required to 'do something' to support those with disability and encourage diversity, even if they are not initially clear on the details of what those requirements are. Most employers are seen to be positive about employing and supporting people with neuro-diversity.

The service has built strong relationships with some larger employers who now take on regular work-placement candidates, some of whom go on to be employed permanently. This placement enables the individual to build up a work history for future employers to see and some work experience, which will benefit them when they look for work elsewhere. Those organisations which demonstrate the most commitment to these programmes often have someone within the company who has a personal link to autism or AS and is able to push the initiative forward. Employers are given AS awareness training before an employee begins working for them.

Good practice for those with AS is also good practice for all staff. Everyone benefits from clarity of communication, written instructions and tasks being broken down into smaller chunks. Managing an employee with AS is excellent experience for a manager, who can develop new skills for themselves in the process. Other potential employees may see that there are benefits in working for a company that has a strong diversity policy and puts its money where its mouth is.

In an ideal world, this level of specialist support would be available to everyone with AS and would help to raise the current, pitifully low employment rate within this group. A person with AS generally only needs quite small adjustments to be able to fully participate and bring unique skills and abilities to the workplace, which would benefit all concerned.

7

How to Make Employment Work – Tips for Success

Communication between employer and employee is essential for the relationship to work. This communication may need to be initiated by the employer, as someone with AS may find it hard to know how to broach the subject, or may find it very difficult to ask for help or admit to having a problem. A structured, regular, scheduled meeting time provides a recognisable, appropriate place for discussions about performance or other work issues.

There are several practical employment support guides available, which provide detailed information on writing CVs, job searching, interview techniques and coping at work. This book has covered these topics briefly. This section presents some more thoughts and considerations on some of the same areas, but is not intended to be comprehensive. It is intended for both the person with AS and their potential employer/ support worker.

Employer / support worker

- Due to the nature of AS, it is especially important for the person with AS to have some level of interest in the work. They may find it impossible to do any job randomly assigned to them.

- Make lists of areas and subjects of interest and explore different job opportunities around these. The person with AS may want to be a computer game designer, but may not have considered all of the other possible job options within the same industry – audio, graphic artist, support technician, character development, cover design, etc.

- People with AS may find it difficult to assess their own abilities and limitations and may agree to take on roles and responsibilities that they do not understand. Some people with AS can be very compliant. Observe and check understanding rather than just asking: 'Do you understand?' (The answer is usually 'yes', to avoid looking a fool, regardless of the truth.)

- High qualifications and/or an impressive CV may not be an accurate measure of whether someone can cope socially or flexibly in a work environment.

- Low or non-existent qualifications and/or a poor CV may not be an accurate measure of intelligence or ability.

- Find another way to assess someone's abilities relating to the actual task that they will be required to carry out, instead of, or as well as, an interview. Asking someone with a verbal communication difference to verbally express their skills and abilities is discriminating on the grounds of their disability. A person with a visual impairment would not be asked to represent themselves visually. This is the same principle.

- If someone with AS is behaving in a way that you consider to be unusual, ask them why. Generally, people don't mind being asked in the spirit of enquiry. This is better than making possibly wrong assumptions about a person's behaviour.

- Identify why the person comes to work – what are their motivators? These may not be as you would expect; not money or status. Working with these motivators will help to ensure the person remains committed and engaged to the job.

- In exchange for strengths in certain skills (systemising, precision and thoroughness), there may be limitations in others (communication skills, flexibility, understanding instructions). Everyone has their strengths and deserves support with their weaker areas.

- If a person has experienced bullying in most of their social interactions, it will take some time before they can trust that any new interaction or association will not be the same. The person with AS may not have had a successful friendship throughout their entire life.

- Be direct with instructions and requirements. Do not wrap up the message with meaningless words. Keep it brief and clear, allowing for no misinterpretations.

- Some people with AS can work very quickly and may need constant challenges to keep their interest. Boredom will lead to lack of motivation and effort.

- When explaining a task, provide the bigger picture. If a person can see where the part of the job they are doing fits into the whole project, this will improve understanding and motivation. If someone perceives their job to be pointless (because no one has explained the point) they may quickly tire. Those with AS like to be useful and productive and not waste their energy on meaningless tasks.

- Provide a suitable workspace, which may be facing a wall or in a separate room. If possible, allow the person to keep the same workspace and not have to hot-desk (use any available desk).

- Be aware that a person with AS may ruminate and go over situations and conversations in their head many times. What may have seemed to be a trivial exchange to you, may cause anxiety and worry over a much longer period for them.

- Be open to the possibility that although their slant may be unusual, the employee with AS may have good ideas and a unique approach to solving problems. Always be willing to reserve judgement.

- Identify tasks which the person with AS can excel at, and do the same for all other members of staff.

- Allow headphones for the person with AS to play music while working, and other sensory adjustments to maintain low stress levels.

Employee

- Having a good knowledge and awareness of AS can be very helpful for being able to ask for what you need. As one person said: 'I find having an understanding of AS helps me to know where I fit in the world, what my skills and weaknesses are, etc.'

- Make a list of all the things that you are interested in and consider what types of job are available in these areas. You will find work much more enjoyable if you want to learn more about what you are doing. Get help from other people to help you come up with broader options.

- Always consider the physical environment (noise, light, smell, etc.) to be a potential stressor if you feel unable to cope at work. Keep a diary to try and isolate the cause of your discomfort, if it is not immediately obvious. It may be that on certain days someone wears a perfume that gives you headaches, for example.

- If you do not wish to 'disclose' officially, it can be easy to get small adjustments without mentioning AS. If you cannot work in a noisy environment, for example, you can say: 'I work much better in a quieter environment, so I'm going to put these earplugs in/listen to some music/move my desk over there'. People are very accepting of this type of assertiveness.

- Many people react very badly to those who cannot make 'normal' eye contact. They perceive someone who cannot 'look me in the eyes' as shifty, deceitful and rude. If you know that this is an issue for you, tell an interviewer, otherwise this could seriously affect your chances of getting the job. Again, this doesn't have to be a disclosure, but perhaps something like: 'By the way, I find it much easier to concentrate when I'm not looking at a person's face, so please excuse me not looking at you very much. I am listening to what you have to say.' This seems a bit odd to say, but, believe me, it works. Once the issue has been brought out into the open, it stops others making wrong assumptions and reacting accordingly (negatively).

- Consider, when you apply for a job, how you will travel to work. Will you be able to make the journey and not be too exhausted or stressed when you arrive? Practise the journey to see how long it takes and what it involves.

- Consider presentation and personal hygiene. Look in magazines and watch how people dress when they are going to work. It is very important to wear the appropriate clothing for the job and to wash and change it regularly.

- Don't be afraid to ask your employer for support if you feel overwhelmed. They are legally obliged to help you and provide what you need (within reason). Find an advocate or get some legal advice if you feel you need it.

- Learning about yourself and recognising the triggers for stress and overload can be very useful for being able to take some time out when you feel these occurring.

- Success or failure in getting a job is only a matter of how good the other applicants were. Most people apply for many jobs that they don't get. It doesn't mean that you are a failure or that you will never get a job. Ask for feedback from the interviewer(s) as to how you could improve your performance.

- Interviews are fake situations. They are not real conversations; they are more like a test in which the correct answers to the questions are not always obvious. Working out what is required can be very difficult. Reading as much about the job roles and organisation as possible may help to give you an idea of the type of company it is – whether they are informal and dynamic or more traditional and structured. This may give you clues as to the type of person they are looking to 'fit' in.

- Success at interviews lies in working out how to answer the questions in the way that the interviewer wants, presenting yourself in the best way possible, without being too honest and without lying. Saying that you were in charge of accounts when you were the only person working in accounts is probably OK. Saying that you were responsible for a multi-million-dollar takeover bid when you actually just ordered the stationery and paid the wages would be a step too far.

- Take the necessary steps to look after yourself at work. Take your breaks alone if you need to and avoid all social invitations if you wish. However, it is worth being aware that other people may assume that you are rude or ignorant if you separate yourself, and this may have an impact on how you are treated at work. This should be your free choice and should have no consequences, but this is not always the case. Going along to the occasional drink after work may help general relationships in the workplace and ensure that colleagues are helpful and cooperative.

Conclusion

Many of the older people among those interviewed had had successful and fulfilling careers with little or no support and often no self-knowledge of AS until later in life. They had to simply get on with it. Younger people with AS have the benefit of early diagnosis and support, so therefore should be even better placed to succeed in work. We have knowledge of AS and other conditions, so there should be no problem in providing the support required. Currently, I am not convinced that this is the case, and the low employment rate backs this up. It has been suggested anecdotally that society has changed and that choice, flexibility and team working are now required skills where perhaps they were less important in times gone by.

The book began with the question: Why are so few adults with AS in employment? From the valuable insights and reports of a number of people with AS, I think that the answer lies at the feet not only of those with AS, but with employers and wider society. Those responding to the questions have made it quite clear what they need in order to be a proficient employee, and these are not big requests: flexibility, a pleasant working environment, some decision-making capability, an interest in their work. These sound like the bare minimum for most people, so not unreasonable demands.

So, if those with AS are willing to work and not making unreasonable demands, then where is the issue, if not with them? The problem, it seems, lies with those making the decisions as to who to employ, how to recruit them and how their jobs should be constructed. There is still a huge lack of awareness of AS and other developmental conditions amongst the general public and this can lead to discrimination. There is such a tendency to make assumptions about certain behaviour – like not being able to look someone in the eyes means you are lying – that it is very hard for many people to step back and look at those assumptions. Unless this changes, there is a high chance of discrimination on the basis of someone's disability, since, in the case of people with AS, these commonly made assumptions are incorrect. Also, the correlation between qualifications and intelligence should be considered with caution, as many people with AS have high academic achievements and others have few or none, and these standards do not necessarily give an accurate picture of intelligence or social and occupational abilities. More knowledge, awareness, training and information on AS is required for all who may be in a position to support or employ those with the condition and provide equal opportunities for them to demonstrate their skills within selection and recruitment and while in work.

What people with AS can do is to make themselves as familiar as possible with their condition and their own strengths and limitations, in order that they can spread the word and increase awareness. Being willing to work at learning new skills in order to create the life you would like to have is your choice and responsibility. It will involve discomfort, change and some anxiety, but this is the only way to make changes – it's the same for everyone. Staying where you are means you will always be where you are. Disclosing and tackling AS may be a daunting prospect, but it can lead to a working life where trying to conceal your differences is not necessary and acceptance of yourself is possible. Prevention is better than meltdown. It is also the path to greater self-confidence, social networks, relationships, new knowledge, doing interesting stuff and having a fulfilling life. Everything is connected, and a movement in one area triggers changes in many others. Try it and see what happens.

Models such as that employed by Specialisterne show that there is a very specific, specialised place where those with AS can find their skills sought after, and although it is not likely that everyone can access such an employer, there must be similar roles in most organisations where someone with AS can be paid to excel at what they are good at. It just takes a little thought. It is quite probable that what someone with AS is good at is something that other employees are less proficient at.

Those who have found successful niches in which their skills are magnified and their limitations shrunk to a manageable size prove that it is possible, and probable, that every person with AS who wishes to find meaningful work can do so.

Last words

For employers: expand your assumptions, get educated and provide the support required to gain a valuable and unique member of your workforce who could have a very positive impact on your business.

For those with AS: you can do it. Get motivated, get out there and show them how good you can be. Ask for the help that you need, and learn about yourself – what makes you excellent and what makes you different. Inactivity changes nothing. Start today!

References

Attwood, T. (2006) *The Complete Guide to Asperger's Syndrome.* London: Jessica Kingsley Publishers.

Barnard, J., Harvey, V., Prior, A. and Potter, D. (2001) *Ignored or Ineligible? The Reality for Adults with Autism Spectrum Disorders.* London: National Autistic Society.

Barnard, J., Prior A. and Potter D. (2000) *Inclusion and Autism: Is it Working?* London: National Autistic Society.

Beardon, L. and Edmonds, G. (eds) (2008) *Asperger Syndrome and Employment – Adults Speak Out about Asperger Syndrome.* London: Jessica Kingsley Publishers.

Health Work Wellbeing Initiative (2008) Healthcare Professionals' Consensus Statement. Statement of Health and Work. 4 March 2008. Accessed on 2 September 2008 at www.workingforhealth.gov.uk/documents/healthcare-professionals-consensus-state ment-4-march-2008.pdf

Hendrickx, S. (2008) *Love, Sex and Long-Term Relationships – What People with Asperger Syndrome Really Really Want.* London: Jessica Kingsley Publishers.

Hendrickx, S. and Newton, K. (2007) *Asperger Syndrome – A Love Story.* London: Jessica Kingsley Publishers.

MacDonald, D. (2007) *Evaluation of the Brighton and Hove ASpire Project, Health and Social Policy Research Centre.* Brighton: University of Brighton.

Meyer, R. N. (2001) *Asperger Syndrome Employment Workbook.* London: Jessica Kingsley Publishers.

Meyerding, J. (2006) 'Coming out autistic at work.' In D. Murray (ed.) *Coming out Asperger – Diagnosis, Disclosure and Self-confidence.* London: Jessica Kingsley Publishers.

Powell, A. (2002) *Taking Responsibility. Good Practice Guidelines for Services – Adults with Asperger Syndrome.* London: National Autistic Society.

Smith, A. and Twomey, B. (2001) 'Labour market experience of people with disabilities. Analysis from the Labour Force Survey of the characteristics and labour market participation of people with long-term disabilities and health problems.' *Labour Market Trends 110,* 8, ISSN: 1361–4819.

Tinsley, M. and Hendrickx, S. (2008) *Asperger Syndrome and Alcohol: Drinking to Cope?* London: Jessica Kingsley Publishers.

Resources

Books

Beardon, L. and Edmonds, G. (eds) (2008) *Asperger Syndrome and Employment – Adults Speak Out about Asperger Syndrome.* London: Jessica Kingsley Publishers.

Fast, Y. (2004) *Employment for Individuals with Asperger Syndrome or Non-verbal Learning Disability.* London: Jessica Kingsley Publishers.

Hawkins, G. (2004) *How to Find Work that Works for People with Asperger Syndrome.* London: Jessica Kingsley Publishers.

National Autistic Society Prospects (2005) *Employing People with Asperger Syndrome: A Practical Guide.* London: National Autistic Society.

Websites

ASpire – mentoring and support for adults with AS in Brighton and Hove. www.aspire.bh-impetus.org

Hendrickx Associates – employer and support service provider for AS training, employment support and advocacy. www.asperger-training.com

National Autistic Society Prospects Employment Service www.nas.org.uk/prospects

The National Autistic Society also has information sheets for employers on supporting employees with autistic spectrum conditions.

Specialisterne – Danish company specialising in employing people with AS. www.specialisterne.dk

Index